MOONWEBS

The Unification Church Insignia

MOONWEBS
Journey into the Mind of a Cult

JOSH FREED

Véhicule Press

MONTRÉAL

Copyright © 1989 by Josh Freed
All rights reserved.

First published 1980.
Dépôt légal, Bibliothèque nationale du Québec
and the National Library of Canada, 1st trimester 1989.

Cover art by Eric Slutsky
Printed by Les Éditions Marquis Ltée

Canadian Cataloguing in Publication Date
Freed, Josh, 1949-
Moonwebs
Bibliography: p.
1st Véhicule edition, with new preface.
ISBN 0-919890-93-8
1. Moon, Sun Myung   2. Segye Kidokkyo T'ongil
Sillyong Hyophoe.   3. Youth — Religious life.
4. Brainwashing.   I. Title.
BX9750.S4F73 1989   289.9   C89-090141-4

Distributed in Canada by
UNIVERSITY OF TORONTO PRESS
5201 Dufferin Street
Downsview, Ontario
M3H 5T8

Distributed in the U.S. by
UNIVERSITY OF TORONTO PRESS
340 Nagel Drive
Cheektowaga, New York
14225-4731

Published by
Véhicule Press
P.O.B. 125, Place du Parc Station
Montréal, Québec, Canada
H2W 2M9

Printed in Canada

For my parents

Acknowledgements

This book would not have been possible without the efforts and action of countless people. Space and memory prevent me from thanking them all.

I received invaluable assistance with both the book and the original newspaper series from editor Mark Wilson, who has lived with this story almost as long as I have. Cynthia Good, Larry Goldstein and the others at Dorset added lots of help, hours and patience to the brew, while Victor Dabby and Bryna Shatenstein have watched lovingly over the project and its author since its inception.

Sheila Fischman and Dawn Macdonald helped to have the book published. Sheila Arnopolous, Marc Raboy, Frieda Miller, my parents and many others suffered bravely through my early drafts. Expertise, ideas and support were provided by numerous people including John Clark, Margaret Singer, Daphne Greene, Mike Kropveld, Sheila Hodgins, Adi Gevins, Gary Scharff, Jay Jaffe and the Maxwells.

Benji was a constant, patient source of information and insight.

Above all, the book owes its existence to Benji's family and dozens of other people in Montreal and San Francisco who took part in the events. Without their courage, dedication and generosity neither this story, nor my account of it, could have occurred.

Preface

In the ten years since *Moonwebs* was first published much has happened in the world of cults — but little has changed. Sun Myung Moon, the unseen antagonist of this book, was sentenced to eighteen months in an American prison on charges of "conspiring to evade income taxes." Since his release he has resumed working toward his stated goal — "to get hold of the whole world."

Moon continues to fund lavish worldwide conferences of influential scientists, media members and politicians; he has added the *Washington Times* to his growing stable of major daily newspapers, as well as a glossy newsmagazine, *Insight*, with a circulation of over one million. His cult's membership continues to flourish. In 1988, Moon presided over a mass wedding of 13,000 people in Korea, where he personally matched thousands of couples who had never met their spouses until their wedding.

Media interest in the Moonies and other cults has faded somewhat in recent years — and many groups prosper in the silence. I receive a steady stream of letters and phone calls from people with family members who have suddenly disappeared into new, often unheard-of sects. Fortunately, groups to educate people about cults have also grown — largely in the wake of the Jonestown massacre: the mass suicide led by Jim Jones that took place in Guyana, shortly after the events recounted in this book. Anti-cult resource and counselling centres now dot North America. Among the most effective is Montreal's Cult Project, an educational centre run by Mike Kropveld, a principal character in *Moonwebs*.

Benji Miller, the protagonist of *Moonwebs*, has long since come to grips with his Moonie history. A physiotherapist, he lives with his wife and children, still grateful for his dramatic rescue ten years ago. In 1988, Benji organized a huge "tenth anniversary" party — a lively night of music, memories, and comic skits thanking the many people who helped him escape from cult life.

As for the author, I've kept a distance from the emotionally exhausting subject of cults in recent years. But re-reading this book for the new edition sent a long chill down my spine. Looking back, the events I describe seem so bizarre and frightening I would hesitate to believe them myself if I had not lived through them. It is partly because of the story's lasting impact that I am glad to see *Moonwebs* re-published. Some of the specific details of Moon's political and financial empire have changed since the book was written. New material has been added to the psychological literature on cults. But I believe that Benji's story and the questions it raises have as much power and relevance today as when the book was first printed. I hope that reading this story can spare others the pain that Benji, his friends and family experienced to learn its lessons.

February 1989

Preface to Original Edition

The events recounted in this book took place in late 1977 and are factual. Part of the story was documented in a six-part newspaper series I wrote for the Montreal Star in early 1978, that brought the Unification Church into the Canadian public eye for the first time.

I decided to enlarge the account into a book because many extraordinary elements of the story remained to be told. As well, questions lingered in the minds of both the public and myself regarding the phenomenon of "brainwashing".

The first part of this book chronicles the story told in the newspaper series, in greater depth and detail. It also includes the results of an extensive, up-do-date investigation into the financial and political empire of Rev. Sun Myung Moon.

The second part of this book looks more closely at the sudden personality transformation of Benji Miller and other Moonies, and tries to relate his experience to other forces in our society. The conclusions represent more than a year of reading, interviews and research on my part, but still only scratch the surface of this long-ignored subject.

Characters, events and conversations in the book have been re-created carefully from numerous interviews and extensive notes that I kept throughout the experience. The last name of Benji "Miller" has been changed to avoid the publicity that intruded on him and his family after the newspaper account. The name of the detective, "Mick Mazzoni", has also been changed. All other names mentioned are real.

The book does not attempt to present "both sides" of the story, only events as they unfolded for Benji, me and others involved with us. I have interviewed numerous cult authorities and ex-members of the Unification Church — but not present members, as I did not want them to know this work was in progress. The Unification Church has used a variety of tactics against those who attempt to write about them.

Overall, this book is an attempt to come to grips with the most remarkable and thought-provoking experience of my life. I do not intend it as a call to outlaw the Unification Church or other cults; only as a small step in helping to understand such groups and the forces that create them.

February 1980.

Prologue

Silently, the young man stood by the dark highway, watching two last stragglers make their way from the tiny roadside bar to a nearby car. As the headlights clicked on, he pressed a bouquet of flowers to his chest and approached hurriedly, forcing a smile onto his weary face.

"Hi! How'd you like to buy some beautiful, fresh roses?" he asked, thrusting the flowers toward the open window, though not so close as to make them easily visible. The man behind the wheel was drunk. He muttered a vile phrase and gunned his car out of the gravel lot, the taillights receding into surrounding blackness. The young man was left alone, holding his flowers in the quiet night.

Behind him, fields of tall grass stretched toward the horizon, shivering in the brisk wind. Motel lights blinked in the distance, and overhead a three-quarter moon was partially obscured by traces of mist. Dawn was not far away. The young man drew his thin cotton shirt to his neck, chilled not so much by the cold as by the sudden stillness.

Slowly, he became conscious of a dull pain that started in his blistered feet and extended up through his knees and thighs. Fatigue pressed down on his eyelids, making his whole body feel extremely heavy, and a wave of confusion and self-pity passed through his mind. He responded to the momentary lapse as though by instinct, forcing his body erect and his eyelids open again.

"*Sleepy spirits,*" he told himself, in silent warning. "Can't let them get to me. Can't! Mustn't let negativity get a foothold...So much to do, so little time. Out spirits...OUT!"

To bolster himself, he focused all thought on the success of the day's Mission. He had done well: rising with the others at seven a.m. to arrange his flowers, then stepping out into the streets of the small western town at nine, to meet the townspeople as they went to work. Throughout the long day he had raced through the streets, visiting every store in town, a great big heavenly smile stretched across his face for everyone to see. And people had understood, buying up his flowers by the dozen, bringing more than $400 over to Father.

There had been only one minor obstacle: the bouncer at the bar who had initially refused him entry. He had convinced the man easily enough by telling him that all flower profits went to ghetto children in a nearby city, an inconsequential deception in light of the urgency of his Mission: building *a better world*.

Now the young man became aware of another growing pain, this time in his stomach. He had eaten little during the day—a liquid fast until noon and a peanut butter and jam sandwich for supper—though he had weakened momentarily and bought a small chocolate bar for dessert. Tomorrow he would be stronger, he told himself in angry admonishment.

Looking up, he saw the lights of a car approaching through the mist, and seconds later a large blue van pulled up before him, its rear doors swinging open. He climbed aboard quickly and heaved a sigh of relief: *back on the track with his brothers and sisters again!*

Inside the van a familiar scene: two of his sisters were busy counting stacks of bills, stuffing them into a brimming canvas bag; a brother clipped the stems off dozens of flowers, trying to prolong their lives another day.

The group had travelled 1,000 miles in the four days since collecting their last flower shipment at the Airport.

Everyone in the van was smiling, and he joined them on

the metal floor, emptying his pockets of bundles of five and ten dollar bills. He could feel the comforting shift of the gears beneath him as the van moved off toward its next destination, a hard three-hour drive; he would have to hurry if he hoped to catch some sleep before his own turn at the wheel in less than two hours.

For the next half hour he helped the others clean the van and count their day's take—more than $2000 among the five of them. Then, without a word, everyone knelt, linked hands, and began to pray.

Eyes closed, the young man began his prayer mechanically, thanking Father for the sun and mountains and the chance he had been given to build a new life. At first his prayer came slowly, by rote—but as he continued, familiar feelings began to rush through him again.

With a growing sense of guilt, he recalled the many sins he had committed during the long day's Mission, particularly his weakness at dinnertime in buying the *chocolate bar*. He had seen it lying on the counter of the grocery store and momentarily lost his resolve, buying it with Father's very own money—money that was to have gone to the task of building *the ideal world*.

And as he dwelt on his sin and recalled the absolute urgency of the Mission, a violent sense of shame and anger began to flood over him. Tears welled in his eyes. At the same time, he became conscious of a growing sound—a rising drumbeat in the air around him—and he joined in instinctively with the others, beating his fists against the van's walls, gently at first, then more and more powerfully as his remorse overcame him.

The world was so terrible and so was he. Father needed him so badly, yet he was still so weak.

He could feel his fists growing red and sore as they pounded more and more furiously at the side of the van, he could feel tears warm on his face, he could hear his own voice growing louder and louder until he was screaming at the very top of his lungs, joining in with the others, crying: "Get out, get out, *get out Satan. Get out of my body, get out of my mind Satan, Satan,* SATAN get OUT. GET OUT! GET OUT! OU-U-U-UUUTTTTTTTT!!!"

Outside, their muffled cries were all that could be heard for miles as the van sped across the silent plain.

Part I

1

The phone at my desk had been ringing for some time, though I'd been trying to ignore it. The evening was busy enough down at the newsroom without further problems: typewriters and telexes were clacking away, nervous editors were rushing about, and I had somehow got mired in an interview with a woman whose daughter had been banned from men's hockey.

On the 14th ring I relented; whoever it was seemed determined to reach me. Reluctantly, I put the hockey mom on hold and moved to the other phone.

The caller was Janet, a good friend of mine, and her message was brief. At last she had heard from Mike, and the news was worse than anyone had expected: he wasn't coming home either—the second friend we had lost in months, to an increasingly eerie chain of events. As Janet sketched the details of Mike's call, my mind skipped backwards, trying to put things in some kind of perspective.

It had started four months earlier when our friend Benji, a young schoolteacher, had left for vacation on the west coast. According to plans, he had spent a week in Vancouver, then headed for California, where he had hoped to visit a cousin on some kind of "commune" near San Francisco. Benji had intended to stay only several days—but something had altered his plans.

Sporadic postcards soon began to extend Benji's vacation, first by weeks and then indefinitely. His only phone call lasted barely a minute and explained little: he seemed remote from family and friends and vague about when, if ever, he planned to return. Instead, he rambled on in a distant tone about his cousin's "fantastic project"—a communal farm where "honest, sincere people" and a remarkable set of "lectures" made for an "exciting new community".

Benji's language was unnerving and very unlike him, but he refused to elaborate by letter or phone; his last postcard said simply that if we wanted to understand the community better, we would have to visit California and "experience" it ourselves.

It was almost four months before one of our friends, Mike, was able to accept Benji's offer. Mike was single and had two weeks off from his job at a home for disturbed children: he decided to spend it checking up on Benji. Janet drove him to the airport, where he had promised to phone her the very next day with a report on Benji. But ten days passed before Janet received her call—and the moment she answered, she knew something was wrong.

Mike's voice had a strange flat quality, Janet said, almost as though he were reading from a script. For a few seconds she had thought it was a bad joke and forced a laugh—but then a mumbo-jumbo of words poured from the phone so uncannily like those of Benji's original call, she could only stare at the receiver in disbelief.

"Incredible project. *Fantastic* people. *Unbelievable revelations"*. And the remarkable lectures, too complicated to explain.

"I know it's hard for you to understand, Janet, but it can't be described in words—you have to *experience* it," Mike had blurted out with sudden feeling. "All I can say is that it's the best thing that's ever happened to me. I'm staying, Janet, I *have* to stay...and you have to trust me."

She didn't. Moments later she and her husband, Lenny, were dialing friends for help—including me.

All we had to go on was the name of the mysterious commune, which Benji had mentioned in an early postcard: the Creative Community Project, with headquarters in a "big house" somewhere on San Francisco's Washington Street. I was the *Montreal Star's* "authority" on fringe groups; I had investigated Silva Mind Control and several local psychics, and had recently done a feature on the chubby guru Maharaj Ji and a "Festival of Light" his organization had staged in Montreal. But I had never heard of the Creative Community Project, and none of my sources on the occult world were able to help.

That evening I called several Zen Buddhists, two well-known psychics, an expert on new religions at a local university, and a couple of Vancouver journalists I knew to be interested in communal groups—but no one knew a thing about the mysterious "project". The files at the newspaper—usually helpful on everything from gumdrops to goblins—didn't turn up a breadcrumb either. At two a.m. I called it a night and went home.

Next morning I scoured press clippings and began calling San Francisco,—but it wasn't until mid-afternoon that I finally hit pay dirt. The *Examiner's* cult expert, Carol Pogash, had just stepped in, and she knew who was behind the elusive project: a group called the "Moonies".

At the time, the word struck only a faint chord in my memory. It was still months before the Guyana suicide would make cults a topic of household conversation, and whatever notoriety the Moonies had thus far earned in the U.S. had yet to cross the Canadian border. I recalled only a few vague details about a rich Korean named Moon who ran a quasi-military group of spaced-out youngsters. I had seen a picture of him in *Time* magazine—a zealot slashing the air with karate chops—but his group had seemed so outlandish that I hadn't even read the entire story.

From Pogash I learned that "Moonies" was a media tag for the Unification Church, a large American cult with a "strange hold" on its young members. Pogash didn't have time to elaborate, but she told me where to look and who to call for information. Before she hung up, she cautioned that we could probably pull Mike out if we hurried, but we had best forget about Benji. It seemed a peculiar thing to hear from an intelligent journalist—but several hours later I could understand her concern. By then I had gathered a file several inches thick on Sun Myung Moon, and if even part of it were true, Benji and Mike were in serious trouble.

According to press reports, Moon was a self-appointed Messiah who combined politics, philosophy and religion in a mission to "conquer and subjugate the world". While he lived in luxury, his young disciples led Spartan, self-sacrificing existences, forsaking everything from cigarettes and alcohol to sex. His North American following alone was said to number 30,000, many of whom were not even aware they were part of Moon's empire.

More disturbing still, the Moonies were under attack from parents, media and ex-followers for "brainwashing" normal young people into "mental slaves". Published reports on the organization read like science fiction.

Members were said to work up to 22 hours a day, reduced to "walking zombies" by exhaustion, protein deficiency and isolation from society. Some psychologists alleged that Moonies were "emotionally frozen", the effects so traumatic that they had permanently dilated pupils. Women members were said to cease menstruating, men to become impotent and even stop growing facial hair.

"It's a horrible, unimaginable process that turns people into robots," said a middle-aged San Francisco pharmacist, named Neil Maxwell, whom we talked to by phone. His own step-daughter had spent five years in "the Church" before he had managed to extricate her, and he was convinced the group was a "menace to humanity".

"I know you'll have a hard time believing me, but when you meet your friends, you'll understand. They won't be the same people...they've cut the pipeline from their guts to their heads."

Compared to the Moonies, the community our friends had left behind was, to say the least, loosely-knit. Benji and Mike had lived in an immigrant quarter around Montreal's legendary "Main", a hodge-podge of ramshackle three-storey dwellings and cluttered, colorful shops that house an assortment of immigrants, French Canadians and aging graduates of the Sixties.

The younger people in the district, including me, formed a community of our own, a mix of community workers, urban activists and unemployed, all somewhat attached to our tattered neighborhood. Still, we were a casual and disorganized bunch. Our only formal group activities were a weekly ball hockey game and a neighborhood food cooperative that was always forgetting to get its shopping done.

The night after Janet's alert, about 25 people gathered at her house for an informal meeting, shaken and bewildered by the strange organization that had swallowed up our friends. Most of us had always assumed that cults were for lost souls and borderline psychotics—not apparently stable and intelligent people. No one could make sense of it, least of all me.

I had known Benji Miller for more than 15 years. He was my oldest friend: a rugged athletic fellow with a receding thatch of light red hair, a bushy beard and the even-keeled temperament of an old sea captain. Since graduating from McGill University with me eight years earlier, Benji had lived a somewhat itinerant life. He'd travelled in Europe for a year, worked with youngsters in Vancouver and Montreal, and spent a year in Africa co-ordinating a teen-age exchange program for the Canadian government.

It had been a free-wheeling lifestyle, but no one who knew him had been the least concerned. Benji was a solid, stable person with few apparent self-doubts and an inner strength that friends looked to during personal crises. A year previously he had returned to school to acquire a teaching diploma and finished near the top of his class. Teaching offers were already arriving in his mailbox when he left for his west coast vacation and his prospects for the coming year had seemed bright.

Benji just wasn't the type to look for easy answers. To him, the cousin he had gone to visit in San Francisco had always been "a bit naive...a guy who likes to dive into spiritual stuff head over heels".

I didn't know Mike as well, but we had a number of friends in common. He'd spent the last four years working with mentally retarded children and adults, a job at which he excelled. He was know as a care-free, gregarious, funny guy with many friends and a steady girlfriend. Just before he'd left to see Benji, Mike had organized a successful union drive at his workplace. Both he and Benji had always been down-to-earth people; neither seemed the type even to visit, let alone get snared by, a messianic religious cult.

The evening's meeting was a sombre affair for a lively group accustomed to gathering only for parties. As we sprawled about the lumpy chairs and fraying carpet of the old flat, people drifted in continuously, as though to an emergency clinic.

"Community organizer, junior college professor, doctor, legal aid lawyer, unemployed," I scribbled into the first of many notebooks I would fill in the weeks that followed, recording the saga toward its uncertain end. "Average age- 28-29. Average income—$12,000. Dress—corduroy pants, jean skirts and baggy sweaters."

People had come to the meeting out of an instinctive concern, though few had much idea of what they faced. The nervous chatter at the start of the evening ended abruptly as we handed out the literature we had collected on Moon. The most disturbing information for most people was the secrecy of the Moon organization: it seemed likely the Unification Church employed numerous aliases that might have been used to deceive our friends.

No other explanation for their involvement really seemed possible, considering Benji and Mike's long-time political and social values. Both were left-leaning humanists with liberal views on both political and social issues, while Moon seemed precisely the opposite. We had obtained a copy of a speech made by Moon during Watergate, in which he had defended Richard Nixon as an "archangel". The speech reflected well the mystical, right-wing tone of Moon's overall politics, while his stance on social issues—such as sex—was almost unimaginable.

"If someone comes and tries to kiss you, bite off his tongue," Moon said in one address to his female followers. "You will be very famous...If a man is killed by biting, then at once the Unification Church will be famous all over the world. Afterwards, no man will attack a sister of the Unification Church."

Moon even seemed to be anti-semitic, though Benji and Mike were both Jewish.

"By killing one man, Jesus, the Jewish people had to suffer for 2,000 years...During the Second World War, six million people were slaughtered to clean all the sins of the Jewish people from the time of Jesus."

It was unthinkable that Mike or Benji could be aware of Moon's doctrines, if they knew of Moon at all: his tenets flew in the face of everything they had always stood for. If they were to read some of Moon's literature, surely both Montrealers would pack their bags and run.

We did not seriously discuss the possibility that our friends had somehow been "brainwashed". The idea seemed too fantastic to merit open discussion. In all likelihood they had simply been duped into staying, caught up in some kind of communal group experience with little idea of who or what was behind it.

We didn't really know what we could do to help, but all of

us were agreed on one course of action: we would send someone to talk with Mike and Benji and warn them of what we knew about the Moon organization. This time however, we weren't going to chance another "experience" like Mike's. Something powerful was obviously at work, so we would send a delegation of people to make sure that everyone we sent came back. The choice was myself, Janet's husband Lenny, and Marilyn, a long-time friend of Benji's. As Janet put it:

"If it's good enough to get all of you...write me a letter, because I'm coming too."

We needed money to finance the trip, and the obvious source was Benji's parents. They had been calling Janet ever since Mike had left for San Francisco, anxious for news of their missing son. But no one wanted to alarm them yet—the situation might be overblown and easily solved. We decided to keep our secret a while longer.

We took up a collection among ourselves, and were all surprised when it totalled some $5,000 in checks and pledges. At 1:30 a.m. the meeting dissolved and we wandered outside into the cool air, where we stood around in small groups exchanging some nervous soul-searching. How well did we really know our two missing friends...what had we missed? Was Benji discontent with the prospect of teaching? Was he anxious about looking for a new job? He wasn't the sort of person to complain about his problems...but maybe some of us should have asked. And what about Mike? Was there something troubling him that none of us had seen?

Most of our questions came to dead ends. Sure Benji and Mike had their share of problems—but fewer than most people we knew, including many of us.

Over the next two days our plans progressed quickly as we booked flight, hotel and car for San Francisco. At the same time, we bolstered our growing arsenal of information on the Unification Church—and the more we learned, the worse we felt. More and more people we talked to warned us that we faced an uphill battle; many told us of alarming personality changes in friends and relatives, some of whom had been sent "underground"—never seen or heard from—for as long as two years. Whatever it was the Moonies did to people seemed to have a powerful and lasting effect.

We also learned of a method of pulling members out of the organization, carried out by specialists referred to as "deprogrammers". But we didn't know who these deprogrammers were, what they did or whether they were any better than the Moonies themselves. Apprehensive, we decided to keep doing things our own way and pushed ahead with our preparations.

The day before we were scheduled to leave, our plans took an unexpected turn when Janet received another late-night phone call from Mike. In a dry, business-like manner, he told Janet that he was returning home for exactly 48 hours to quit work and settle his affairs. Then he was returning to the Creative Community Project "for good".

"People here say I shouldn't go back to Canada, even for a visit. They say my *foundation* isn't good enough," he added suddenly in a quavering voice. "But I'm coming anyways. Pick me up!"

The following day, we burned up the phone lines to half a dozen cities, trying to prepare ourselves for Mike's return. We spoke to ex-members, parents of current members and people who worked for "anti-cult" groups across the U.S. Person after person warned us that they never heard of friends or family successfully talking someone out of a cult like the Moonies. All insisted that there was only one way: deprogramming.

The word alone gave me chills, conjuring up pictures of electrodes and frontal lobotomies. The telephone voices assured us that it was just "a simple talk session", but none of us was prepared to bring in strangers. And though everyone we spoke with was convinced that Benji would require a formal "deprogramming", some were optimistic about Mike.

"Mike's indoctrination might still be weak...Maybe you can do it yourself," said the encouraging voice of the San Francisco pharmacist, Neil Maxwell. "A combination of love and good old common sense might just break their hold on him. Give him love and care...and no matter what happens, don't give up."

We decided to give it a try. Janet, Lenny and a third friend, a psychology teacher, agreed to form the "talk team", while others in the neighborhood would stand by in case support was needed. Maxwell had warned us that Moonies often travel with "shadows"—fellow Moonies who accompany them at all times—so we formed a squad to deal with one if he arrived. We nicknamed it the "souvlaki squad", after a Greek dish sold in the community. Its assignment: "take the shadow out for a souvlaki, whether he wants one or not."

That night Janet and Lenny lay awake in bed with their two-year old son and mulled over Maxwell's final warning: "When you see your friend, don't be shocked if he doesn't look like the same person. He probably won't be the Mike you knew."

When the three-person "talk team" met Mike at the airport next day, they were immediately jarred. Physically, he was himself, apart from a gaze that seemed to focus on a point ten feet beyond them. Emotionally however, he was squeezed dry of much of his normal personality, almost as though he had vacated his mind and someone else had moved in. Usually gregarious, Mike showed none of his characteristic vitality and humor; he spoke in a toneless, aloof manner and had apparently altered many of his former beliefs.

During the drive home, the longtime agnostic railed at his friends with a one-hour lecture about Satan, Messiahs and evil serpents. He was certain that "evil forces" ruled the earth, including his friends, while "good" existed only at the Creative Community Project.

"I hope you understand," he said flatly in a near-alien vocabulary and a calm, reasoned voice, "I've been given a chance to help save the world...to redeem myself from evil."

When they arrived home, Lenny went straight to the study and produced the stack of material we had collected on Moon, dropping it wordlessly before Mike with a thud. But Mike's face remained impassive.

"Newspapers," he smiled knowingly. "I know about them. They don't know what they're talking about...they've only got part of the *whole picture.*"

"But Mike, you've been reading them for years—"began Lenny.

"I'm sorry—you can't possibly understand," Mike broke in, with an air of detachment. "You haven't been there...you have to *experience* it to understand."

The next ten hours were the most frustrating of their lives. Mike apparently didn't know he was in the Unification Church, although he said the organization had come up in one of the last lectures as having some "affiliation" with the Creative Community Project. But it hardly mattered. Mike wouldn't listen to the first word anyone had to say and he believed them even less: he refused to so much as glance at the information we had gathered.

For hours his friends talked, shouted and cried at him, but they might as well have been speaking a foreign language. Mike was without emotion and impenetrable, practically catatonic but for the stream of repetitious garble about "evil forces" that flowed from his mouth like a tape recording.

"Mike's still in there someplace...he's got to be," Janet repeated to herself all night, wanting to believe it. But at three a.m. when she phoned people in the waiting community with a progress report, all she could say was: "God...I don't know if we'll ever be able to get him out."

At breakfast the debate continued, as a glimmer of expression began to crack the armor in Mike's voice offering some hope to his wearying opponents. But then he decided to break off for the afternoon and trotted outside. As they anxiously watched Mike disappear down the stairs, all were tempted to call in the souvlaki squad and restrain him, but they decided he was free to make his own choice. The day was long and nerve-wracking.

At suppertime Mike was back, ambling into the house in more casual fashion and astonishing them with word that he "might" stay longer than the ordained two days. Then he dug into a plate of spareribs, eating with gusto for the first time since his return. By the end of the meal he had agreed to talk with an ex-Moonie in New York, a woman who had spent more than five years in Moon's organization.

That phone call was the turning point. Over the telephone, the woman quickly convinced Mike that the Creative Community Project was part of Moon's empire. Her tales of deception and greed, bolstered by first-hand experience, seemed to jolt Mike's mind out of a deep freeze.

The phone call lasted only an hour, but everyone listening nearby could sense the whole idea turning around in Mike's head like a large tanker slowly changing directions at sea.

"No...no...I don't think I'll be going back," he said unexpectedly at the end of the call, as the others restrained cheers of relief. "It looks like I've got a lot of thinking to do."

In the days that followed Mike steadily returned to his usual self, as though returning from a dream world. His story came out in dribs and drabs.

He had stayed in a camp in the country called Boonville, and knew nothing of Moon or the Unification Church, only an independent group called the Creative Community Project. The camp had been the most intense experience of his life, "crazy, but sincere." Wild enthusiasm. Hundreds of "genuine" people. Strange, stimulating lectures. No time or space to be alone.

"I started out critically...a lot of things bothered me. At first they called me 'Mr. Negativity'...but then I seemed to lose perspective. Everything seemed so real...so spontaneous...so honest.

"My own changes worried me...I kept meaning to leave, get time to think—but somehow they always convinced me to stay 'one more day'. They're very persuasive people."

Close relationships developed quickly through intense personal conversations: days were emotionally draining and mentally exhausting. By the third day he felt like "an emotional tennis ball...so many ideas and questions...my mind was swimming I thought it would burst."

On the morning of his fourth day in Boonville, Mike had woken up to perceive things with a "new clarity". "My doubts were fading—somehow seemed very unimportant against the grand scheme of the Project. My family had friends seemed so far away..."

It was obvious he should stay in Boonville, and became more and more obvious each day—even though an urge to return home one last time gnawed inside him.

"I was told to forget you guys, forget everything I'd done. I almost did...but somehow I had to come back and explain. I'm just stubborn, I guess...and awfully lucky."

Three days later Mike began to feel an anger that would continue to grow:

"Looking back I can't believe what I let them get away with," he told us "They lied to me in so many ways, but more strangely...I can't figure out why I bought the lies, why I didn't ask questions the way I usually do. Something came over me, destroyed my critical thinking. I just wasn't my normal self at all.

"I think I was brainwashed—that's all I can call it—and Benji's in a lot deeper than I ever was. If we don't get him out of there soon...we're never going to see him again."

2

From the air, San Francisco seemed to twinkle at us like the jewels of a glamorous but deadly woman. Then our plane dipped and plunged toward the glimmering water below, coasting to a landing on a runway that jutted out like a giant pier into the sea.

I had convinced my newspaper editor to grant me a week to investigate Benji's situation. Lenny could not make the trip, but I was accompanied by Marilyn, a lanky, energetic woman who was close to Benji, having lived next door to him for the year before he left. The two had become good friends, just kindling a romance at the time Benji left on holiday. We hoped he would be happy to see us again, regardless of his relationship with the Project.

Mike had given us a telephone number for Benji's house on Washington Street, and we called from an airport phone booth. A sweet, female voice answered on the first ring, chirping "Creative Community Project"; she said Benji was out, but promised he would call our hotel room the moment he returned.

Soon, Marilyn and I were riding across the sprawling five miles of Bay Bridge into Berkeley, the area that would be home and headquarters for days to come. Known to many as Berzerkly, the legendary college town struck us as a jumble of "gourmet ice cream" parlours, hot bagel shops and outdoor hashpipe stands, populated by a sidewalk parade of eccentric characters and motorized wheelchairs.

But the hottest item for sale was undoubtedly salvation, as dozens of sidewalk spiritualists vied for our souls: Krishnites, bible-belters, foretellers of doom and gloom, and members of a variety of centres for "being", "learning" and "loving"; even Otis, our middle-aged black cabbie, had to hurry home so he and his wife could catch their weekly EST session.

The most striking guru we met was the "Prophet of Hate"—an emaciated fellow with a bathing cap and a thin swatch of black material draped over his otherwise naked body—who balanced on one foot in the centre of a water fountain.

"I hate you all...every one of you!!" he shouted to passersby from his odd pedestal, while a nearby guitarist played classical jazz in the background. "I used to love everyone...but it didn't work...so now I hate instead. I hate you!...I HATE you all!!"

Several hours after our arrival, Marilyn and I checked into a room in a small Berkeley Hotel. We showered, and were just unpacking our bags, when we received a brief phone call from Benji. He sounded wary, and surprised to hear from us, but he was apparently pleased that we were in town. He said he could not speak to us then, as he was rushed and calling from a pay phone; nor could he see us that evening. But he promised to spend the following day giving us a tour of San Francisco—then cut the conversation short to rush to a "meeting".

We spent our free evening with Neil Maxwell, the pharmacist who had been so helpful over the phone in advising us on Mike. The man proved equally amiable in the flesh: a portly, middle-aged fellow with a piece symbol on his belt and a chipmunk smile flashing between craggy features and a greying beard. He and his soft-spoken wife, Anne, lived in a cluttered bungalow in Berkeley that was a virtual way-station for those battling Moon; throughout our visit ex-Moonies came and went, and the phone rang regularly with appeals from parents of youngsters still in the cult.

The Maxwells spent several hours a day offering parents advice on Moon's organization and the psychological impact it had upon its members. In return for their help, they asked for little—a $25 contribution for the "cause", and even that was strictly voluntary. Yet their generosity was not difficult to understand, once we had heard their story.

The couple had seen their own daughter fall under Moon's spell for almost five years, gradually losing contact with her entirely, until they had made the most difficult decision of their lives and dragged her out to be deprogrammed. They had never regretted the choice. For five days, the young woman had lain on their living room floor in the fetal position, rocking back and forth and refusing to speak or even open her eyes. Her parents had to carry her to the toilet. When their daughter finally agreed to discuss her involvement with Moon, a deprogrammer needed only two days to convince her to abandon the organization forever. More than two years had passed since the young woman had made her decision to leave; now she was happily settled in New York, completing graduate studies.

"The Moonies are very selective about the kids they take," Maxwell explained to us, during a busy evening on the telephone. "They want them bright and well-educated, yet sensitive to outside pressure and logic. It's best when they're in periods of transition—from jobs, school or relationships. Everyone is in transition sometimes...and that's when the Moonies like to strike."

Maxwell had never been to the Boonville camp himself, but he was convinced it was a frightening "mind trap" that robbed bright, responsive young people of their entire emotional spectrum. Somehow, he explained, it locked people into a mental state that allowed "no personality development as long as they stay in...just like a deep freeze."

Only one piece of information cheered our spirits: according to Maxwell, the deep freeze worked both ways. "If your friend was pretty much together when he went in, he'll be pretty much together when he comes out. Don't worry," he added gently at the evening's end. "See Benji a few times...build his trust in you as friends. Sooner or later you'll get through to him."

The advice was comforting, so we returned to our hotel room about two a.m. to get some sleep. But several hours later, an early morning phone call interrupted both our sleep and our plans.

"Something's come up," said a slow voice on the other end of the line, in a tone so bloodless I shivered. It was Benji. Before I could say a word in reply, I heard him recite the address of a restaurant, and instruct me to be there in half an hour. Then he hung up.

Soon afterwards, Marilyn and I were sitting in a tiny San Francisco coffee shop, staring at orange vinyl booths and a doughty waitress who demanded our order. We forced our way through several coffees and a string of donuts to keep the table, increasingly uncertain whether our friend would be there. It was more than an hour after our arrival when he finally appeared—though the pallid, expressionless figure that walked through the door bore almost no resemblance to the person we had known.

Benji's beard had been shaved, his hair was closely cropped and his robust body had turned pale and emaciated; he appeared to have lost about 30 pounds. Yet far more disturbing was the look on his face, for his eyes had a flat and lifeless quality, and the smile that clung limply to his lips bore no apparent connection to the person beneath. His overall expression was so blank that he could have been lobotomized—and as I glanced at Marilyn, I could see she was as astounded as me.

Yet both of us had to suppress our shock, for Benji had not come alone. Three other people arrived with him—two of them holding his hands—and before we could say a word, they plumped down to join us at the tiny restaurant table. All, we soon discovered, were members of the Creative Community Project; and they identified themselves as Benji's new "family".

The most talkative of the three was Bethie, an effervescent yet earthy young woman of 28, who had black hair tied back in a pony tail and a radiant, piercing smile. "You look like a lot of my friends," she told me almost immediately, staring warmly into my eyes. "I have the feeling that I've known you for a *long* time."

Flanking Benji's other side was Matthew, an earnest-looking fellow with short blond hair and a drab 1960s sports jacket; he told us that he had been a forest ranger, before joining the "family" some five years earlier. At the far edge of the table sat Kristina, a silent but striking brunette in her late thirties who was introduced as a psychologist. She was a stern-looking matron, with intelligent eyes that scrutinized us closely, and she doled out regular smiles like a doctor offering medication. Throughout the meal, other family members also drifted in and out of the restaurant, stopping by to say hello.

Everyone we met seemed intelligent and likeable, though their conversation was always related to the goals and achievements of the Creative Community Project. Farms, houses, shops and clinics: they rattled off enough holdings to impress a banker. The group even had plans to build a free school, and "possibly" a university. Their "project" seemed to be a mix between a sixties-style commune and a modern land-development corporation; and it would have made for compelling discussion, if not for one increasingly alarming aspect.

Throughout the conversation, Benji took no part whatever, gazing silently across the room as though he were in some kind of trance. The warmth, wit and camaraderie I had known for 15 years were completely absent, and his hands were held almost continuously by at least one family member. He did not ask a single question about family or longtime friends, and when I brought them up, he didn't seem remotely interested; all he would repeat were occasional wooden phrases like: "It's—really great to see you. It—really—is."

Bethie salted his eggs, put sugar in his coffee and even cut his food for him; if I asked him a question, she would answer it herself with a disarming smile as Benji stared off into space. Despite the stories we had heard, Marilyn and I could not believe our eyes. Frozen between utter disbelief and fear of giving ourselves away, we struggled simply to make eye contact with our distant friend.

A half hour into the encounter, Kristina smiled, then left, pausing outside to sketch a mysterious circle on the window for Bethie to see. Minutes later, Bethie interrupted the meeting to inform us that Benji would have to leave on a "family project", and might be gone for several days. He nodded passively in assent.

"What project?" I asked him point-blank, stunned to realize that we might not see him again. We had hardly exchanged fifty words.

"Well...I'm not sure exactly...we have lots of projects everywhere," he replied in a detached monotone, gazing slightly by me. "Maybe I'll see you before you leave."

Both Marilyn and I pressed him to spend more time with us; we would be in town for only one week, and who knew when we might see him again? It was an emotional appeal, and for a moment, Benji seemed to respond with warmth, looking directly at Marilyn for the first time since he had arrived. But Matthew whispered something in his ear, and his eyes became remote again.

"What I have to do is very important," droned Benji. "More important than what I feel like doing. You'll have to understand."

Suddenly, Bethie announced that it was time to leave, and Benji instantly began to rise. As he did so, Marilyn broke in, visibly distraught: "Benji...we came 4000 miles especially to see you. You *can't* just leave. What do you have to do thats so important, it can't wait for a few more hours...what's going on here?...Who *are* these people?"

Again our friend seemed to waver, his eyes searching

Marilyn's face as though trying to place someone he had not seen in years; but Bethie whispered something to Matthew, who quickly opened the restaurant door. Then she touched Benji's arm lightly.

"Come on Benji, we gotta go," Bethie smiled; and from the immediate shift in Benji's expression, there was little doubt that our meeting was over.

"You'll have to understand," Benji droned again. "I'm sorry...I have a community responsibility. I have to go."

Bethie and Matthew each took one of his arms and escorted him outside like an old man, leaving Marilyn and me speechless in the restaurant doorway. The whole encounter seemed impossible, unfathomable; I had known Benji for years, but this just wasn't him. Some kind of overwhelming guilt or obligation seemed to be fencing him in like a cage—but what was it? And how had they gained such horrifying control?

Through the window, we could see the three of them piling into a waiting Volkswagen and we rushed out onto the busy sidewalk toward the car's open window. Benji's room would be empty while he was gone, I pointed out as I heard the car engine start; could I stay there until he returned?

Benji had never turned down a stranger, let alone a good friend, in his life—but now he could only look helplessly toward Bethie to see what he should do. She smiled, and recommended the Salvation Army around the block "for only five dollars". Then she leaned out the car window, smiled cheerfully at me, and added:

"Come to the house on Washington Street for supper tonight. I'm expecting you." As she spoke, their car pulled abruptly from the curb.

Two hours later, Marilyn and I knocked nervously at the door of a well-known San Francisco deprogrammer. We had phoned Neil Maxwell for help, and as a last resort, he had recommended we seek more qualified aid. We took his advice; although we still had no intention of "deprogramming"

Benji, we badly needed clues to his new mentality if we were ever going to get through to him ourselves.

The deprogrammer was a swarthy Malaysian named Tony Gillard. He was tall and heavy, about 30 years old, with a handlebar moustache and a sinister appearance that contrasted oddly with soft, gentle manners. He was very sympathetic.

"Your friend is under a very sophisticated form of psychological control...made to feel guilty about everything in him that's human," he explained. "He's been told that you're evil, and he has to resist you. The more he feels attracted to you, the *weaker* he thinks he is. His whole world is ass-backward.

"I can't explain it fully...but it all happens at Boonville," he added, perceiving our confusion. "That's where you really get messed up. Take my word for it, I used to be a Moonie too."

Briefly, Tony told us his story. It was the first of many we would hear in San Francisco, and all would have a similar theme.

Before he met the Moonies, Tony had run a small but profitable cab company and owned an expensive condominium apartment. He had sold both and turned the money over to the Unification Church, upon joining the group.

His harrowing year in the Project was a dazed, surreal journey in which he was convinced to sacrifice food, sleep and health for Moon and his "Church".

"I worked twenty hours a day, travelling from city to city raising money for Moon...eating the odd sandwich and getting weaker and sicker every day," he recalled. He developed a skin rash that is common to many Moonies, but his superiors instructed him to ignore it, and infection set in. "It turned green with gangrene...but they told me it was the devil, and I believed them. I'd have believed anything they said in my state of mind."

As the infection spread through his leg, Tony said, he

became delirious, terrified of dying on one hand and breaking faith on the other. His sanity drifted away, and he tried to kill himself with an overdose of drugs—winding up instead in hospital, where he remained for several months. That was how the horrible voyage had ended two years previously; now, fully recovered, he was studying for an MA in psychology and working to deprogram others from the Church.

"Cool it," he told us, after hearing the account of our breakfast with Benji. "Kristina and Bethie are very important people in the California Church...that means Benji must mean a lot to them. He's probably being groomed as leadership material."

Tony seemed sure that Benji was somewhere in the area, and he advised that we do our best to wait him out. In the meantime, he gave us more reading material on Moon, and cautioned us to stay on good terms with the rest of the Moonies until we managed to see Benji alone.

"Go to supper at the Moonies' house, act friendly, and maybe they'll bring him out of the closet in the hope of sucking you in too. Then you pull out your information, and spring the bear trap."

The Creative Community Project's house on Washington Street, in downtown San Francisco, was a four-storey manor housing 19 people in a labyrinth of rooms. I left my shoes at the door in a pile of hundreds and signed in with a smiling girl at the door.

"Hi...I'm Janice!" chirped a bouncy young woman as she grabbed my hand and hauled me into a vast dining room with little furniture. Almost 100 people were strewn about the floor, talking enthusiastically and munching on a murky carrot and cabbage stew; it lived up to Tony Gillard's description of "something that looks like it came from the butt of a donkey."

Most people there were "family" members, but a number were "recruits" like me. They had been picked up casually at the bus or train stations by members of the opposite sex, then invited to dinner for a look at an "interesting" project. Several carried suitcases or knapsacks.

Family members were clean-cut and neatly dressed, exuding a warmth that seemed sincere and open. Women were almost uniformly stocky, cheerful and energetic, with names like Muffy, Debby, and Poppy; the men subdued and strangely humorless, often bearing biblical names like Noah and Jeremiah. Some members seemed dazed, with dull eyes and a flat smile, particularly more recent members; those who did the talking however, were gregarious, articulate and likeable.

"Benji's such a great guy," I heard time and again. "You must be a real good guy too." But no one seemed to be able to tell me where he was or when he would return.

Enthusiastic members recited the usual litany of "projects" they were involved in, ranging from farms and clinics to a carpet-cleaning business. "All that in just seven years ...and we've got so much more planned for the future," beamed Janice, giving my captive hand a gentle squeeze. "And wait till you see our farm!"

Recruits were confined to the first floor of the house, though I prowled up the back stairs to see dozens of sleeping bags crammed into floorspace on the upper levels. The downstairs public portions of the house were spacious and well-equipped, including kitchen facilities suitable for a medium-size restaurant.

Dinner was followed by songs, music and pantomime skits. It was a funky, enjoyable show and ended with the whole crowd clapping hands and shouting a kind of self-mocking *"Ya-a-ayyyy!"*

Into the center of this cheer strode our matronly breakfast companion, Kristina, looking radiant and far more affable than earlier in the day. As she passed, my supper partner Janice reached out, closed her eyes and hugged Kristina's leg, murmuring: "Oh Kristina! It's so wonderful to see you again!" Kristina returned a perfunctory smile, mussed Janice's hair and moved to the front of the room—where rows of chairs had been set up for the evening "lecture". Silence immediately gripped the room, and Kristina began to speak.

"Most people have convinced themselves that the best they can do in life is to make sure they're not too unhappy," she explained. "Pretty soon, they start to believe that that's what happiness really is...just not being *un*happy.

"It's called learning to compromise—the don't-bug-me-man, I'm-*happy*-being-unhappy mentality."

Kristina's lecture mixed history, science and philosophy with a steady dose of psychology; ideas wheeled by so fast I could hardly recall them. One moment Kristina had a rose in her hand, casually yet humorously listing its intricate parts by their Latin names; the next, she was telling us a jived-up version of the Project's favorite parable, the wise men and the elephant, to drive home the point that to "understand life, you've got to have the *whole picture*...not just a part of it."

The lecture was silly but engaging. Kristina was remarkably persuasive, and she bounded around imitating everything from a rock to a hungry elephant, giving a spontaneous cover to what struck me as a carefully honed and polished lecture. I was sorry when the performance ended an hour later coming to an engaging close with a deliberately corny parable:

"Stephen comes home hungry, clutching his stomach, dr-a-gs himself into the kitchen...and there...is the roast beef. There are precisely three things he can do—

"First...he can eat-all-the-roast-beef-himself (she pantomimes stuffing a roast hurriedly down her throat).

"Second...he can cut a slab, and leave the rest for everyone else. Or third...he can make a huge, fantastic sandwich for everyone...the whole world...with (as she builds the invisible sandwich, layer by layer) ham, cheese, bananas, raspberries, avocados, jelly, chocolate cake, and...a cherry on the top. A FORTY FOOT SANDWICH...held together ingeniously...by the *mayonnaise* on the bottom of each slice.

"Because (voice rising) Stephen is conscientious of not

only himself...but others around him. He wants to *share*. And that's our philosophy here at the CCP. We want to share —not just with our friends, that's not good enough— but with the whole world. And if you don't believe me... look around you at what we've done, then come out to Boonville for a visit to our model community.

"Even the cows look happy there...it's the greatest place on earth!"

Seconds later we were watching a slide show of Boonville Training Camp, where Mike had received his indoctrination. It looked lovely: a 650-acre retreat with grassy fields, quiet creeks, woods, sports, wholesome guys and pretty girls—an ideal vacation site for a traveller on his or her first trip to California.

As well, the farm offered a two-day "seminar" and a chance to see their "model community" at work. The cost was $18 for room and board; in exchange, we were promised the "most remarkable two days" of our lives. Moon and the Unification Church were never mentioned during the entire evening—only the Creative Community Project.

Buses were leaving for Boonville soon after, and Janice squeezed my hand and encouraged me to come, "for me". I didn't, as I was determined to stay in San Francisco until Benji reappeared—but some 30 family members and 8 recruits prepared to leave for the camp soon afterwards. Many of the recruits were students and vacationing young people from other countries, caught up by the unusual activities of the evening and looking for a stay in the country. Others, like Benji and Mike before them, had come to the house to visit friends in the family, and were going up to Boonville to see what their buddies were doing.

Coffee was served, and soon Bethie and a serious fellow named Bruce were applying the screws for me to go to Boonville as well. The seminar was "just beginning"; it was the "perfect time", Bruce urged gently. "It's good to go while you're in the mood...it's been our experience that later, people get lazy. What else do you *really* have to do?"

My dinner mate, Janice, went slightly overboard with her spiel, singing me a few bars of:

"We love you Jo-o-osh, Oh yes we do-ooo.
We don't love anyone, as much as you-ooo."

But she quickly wilted under an icy stare from Bethie, who seemed to know that such cornball antics were not the way to entice me to Boonville. Instead, Bethie took a more tactful approach; she suggested that if I were to go up to Boonville—"Who knows"—Benji "might" show up too.

I resisted her bait. I was determined to stay in San Francisco until Benji appeared rather than see him in Boonville surrounded by dozens of other Moonies. And underlying this reason for refusing the invitation was another: I was apprehensive about the effect the Boonville camp might have on me.

As I left Washington Street house a few minutes later, a full moon peered through the clouds like a watchful eye. It was the first full moon of late September, the Harvest Moon. In its light, other recruits from the house were already boarding a bus marked "Elephant Express", their arms linked with Project members of the opposite sex.

Everyone looked as if they were heading for a fun weekend in the country, and I could see why. To the unsuspicious eye, the night's performance might have seemed spontaneous, unusual and even enticing. I was thankful I had known of the Creative Community Project and its activities before I arrived.

Marilyn and I remained in San Francisco for two weeks, growing more frustrated each day. We called the family every day, but came no closer to seeing Benji; according to Bethie, he was "impossible to reach"; he would probably be back "in a matter of days" but there was "no way" of knowing for sure. In the meantime, she said, why didn't we come and spend some time at Boonville?

Nor were we alone in our trials. We learned that eight sets of parents were also in town, trying to make contact with

Moon-struck kids. Some were from Canada and the eastern U.S., others from as far away as Britain and Australia; yet all had stories that were carbon copies of our own. They were seeking, bright, well-educated and "normal" youngsters who had virtually cut off communications since visiting Boonville.

There was even a Canadian Cabinet Minister in town, attempting to retrieve his former executive assistant from the Moonies. The man was Norm Cafik, then Minister of State (Multiculturalism), and he was looking for a 21-year old whiz kid whom he described as "one of the brightest and most capable young people around Ottawa, a super guy, whom everybody liked and respected."

The youngster had been on vacation from law school when he had been swallowed up by the California Project; and though the Minister had spent several months preparing himself for his "rescue trip" west, he had found his one encounter with his aide "the most traumatic experience of my life."

"He wasn't the person I had known," a distraught Cafik told me in a phone conversation. "He was just a shell of his former self. I thought I could reach his intellect—but from what I could see the group treats intellect as the next thing to a criminal offence."

Legally, there was not much that the Minister, or any of us could do. A recent California Court judgement involving the Moonies had ruled, on grounds of religious freedom, that parents had no right to intervene. If an adult did not wish to see his family again, there was nothing a parent could legally do.

Frustrated, many parents had turned to Neil Maxwell and others like him—a loose-knit coalition of people trying to battle Rev. Moon. We met several of them during our stay in California, a varied lot that included Maxwell, Tony Gillard and a young Protestant minister who had sensed "evil ...smothering you like a blanket" the one time he visited the Moonie house.

Another opponent of the Moonies took a direct approach.

He was a college student who had lost a close friend to the group several months earlier; now he frequently picketed Washington House with a sign warning: "GUESS WHO'S COMING TO DINNER? THE POWERFUL SUN MYUNG MOON AND HIS CORPORATE EMPIRE." It was an effective tactic scaring off many newcomers who did not know of the link between Moon and the Project—so effective that the Moonies re-scheduled their dinners to avoid the young man's visits.

Without doubt the most dazzling opponent of Moon was Daphne Greene, a middle-aged housewife who was the virtual motor of California's anti-Moon forces. A tall, articulate and commanding woman, she had lost two children to Moon in six months, prompting her to leave a post at the University of California to study Moon and his empire full-time.

Since that time, she had amassed a sea of data on Moon's organization. In her spacious mountaintop home on the outskirts of San Francisco, filing cabinets brimmed and cupboards overflowed with information on Moon's immense holdings; even the walls of her home were covered in winding flow charts of Moon's maze of corporate ties. We learned from Mrs. Greene that the U.S. government had also launched an investigation into Moon's murky political network. The investigating committee was headed by Rep. Donald Fraser, and a report was due in several months. But for Daphne Greene, the verdict was already in.

"Moon's businesses change names and locations faster than a floating crap game," she maintained. "It's not a church, it's a business operation, and the kids are just slaves who make it work."

Mrs. Greene and the others offered information, guidance and sympathy to worried parents, but in the final analysis, there was little they could do to get unwilling children out of the cult. For some parents, this was simply not enough, and they took the law into their own hands. We heard dozens of stories about parents who had kidnapped their own children, in pandemonic scenes that resembled movie scenarios. One family had apparently driven into Boonville, grabbed their daughter and sped off toward the Canadian border, with a carload of Moonies close behind. An elderly mother had wrestled her teen-age son to the floor and poured out her feelings until he agreed to talk; and some parents had rented ex-marines, private police and even helicopters to stage dramatic rescues that led to days of forced deprogramming.

Many of these were amateur efforts with little assistance, others were slick affairs run by seasoned pros. Some deprogrammers ran a virtual business, charging thousands of dollars to kidnap and deprogram Moon-struck kids. The most well-known of these was a former boxer named Ted Patrick, who had grabbed and deprogrammed some 1500 youngsters from dozens of cults, and had already spent time in jail for kidnapping.

We met a young assistant of Patrick who was in town on a "Moonie case". He carried an attache case full of plastic handcuffs and was well armed with mace. He spoke of "smacking 'em around to make 'em listen", and offered us his services for a hefty fee.

Marilyn and I were repelled by this young man and his methods, but it was not hard to see why many parents might go along; the alternative seemed far worse. The two of us spent two weeks in San Francisco and exhausted a dozen strategies trying to see Benji; none had the slightest effect.

Local police wished us good luck, but were powerless to help. They said several other Moonies had disappeared in identical fashion, but the law gave them no right to intervene. U.S. immigration officials were equally sympathetic and equally ineffective: true, Benji was residing in the U.S. illegally, but it might take years to deport him—if we could locate him.

And the Canadian Consulate had nothing to add. "Our hands are tied," was the official position, though one young consular official took us aside and told us: "If I were you, I'd buy wire cutters and binoculars, sneak into Boonville, grab your friend and head for Canada."

As we entered our second week in San Francisco, we concocted even more elaborate schemes to see our friend. We distributed Benji's photograph to San Francisco buddies and set up stake-outs outside several Moon homes; we sent mock recruits to dinner at Washington house to snoop around for signs of Benji. We even schemed with a sympathetic local doctor to have Marilyn hospitalized, in hopes that her feigned illness might draw Benji out. Nothing worked.

On our 13th day in town, Marilyn made a last desperate attempt. She stormed dramatically into Washington house and told several Moonies that she had stored Benji's belongings at her home in Montreal—including an expensive stereo system. It was taking up much-needed space, she complained, and she had to consult Benji before she left San Francisco the following morning.

"If he can't be bothered to at least make a phone call ...then I'm tossing everything off the balcony," she announced to the startled Moonies, then stomped out the door in a huff. It was our final gambit, and she hurried back to our hotel room to see if Benji would bite.

An hour later, the phone rang—but instead of Benji, it was Lenny in Montreal. Benji's mother had just phoned him in confusion, to say her son had called her: something about picking up some of his belongings from Marilyn's house. Did Lenny know where she could find Marilyn, or a key to her apartment?

We were stunned. The Moonies seemed to have all the bases covered; it had taken less than an hour for the supposedly incommunicado Benji to learn of Marilyn's threat, then call his mother so she could call Lenny and Lenny call us. It was painfully clear that the "family" was going to keep Benji underground as long as we remained in San Francisco; and equally clear that we had reached a dead end.

After consulting with our friends in Montreal, we decided to scrub the mission and return to Montreal: we would have to tell Benji's parents of their son's predicament, and leave the next step up to them.

Before leaving San Francisco, I had a couple of things to do. I accepted Bethie's invitation to visit the mysterious Boonville camp: apprehensive yet determined to see what had turned my lifelong friend into a total stranger. But first, I went to Daphne Greene's files to find out all I could about Sun Myung Moon.

3

A gigantic crimson-carpeted gymnasium in Seoul, Korea, 1974. 1800 young grooms in dark suits kneel beside their 1800 respective brides, most of them complete strangers, dressed in identical white gowns. A chunky Korean in a gold and white robe and silver crown ascends to the pulpit and in a piercing voice pronounces them "Couples...Forever!!"

The White House, late 1973. President Nixon, besieged by Watergate, has virtually barricaded himself inside the Oval Office, as the press, public and much of Congress howl for his resignation. Outside his residence, 1500 neatly shorn young people line up in silence and on command, fall simultaneously to their knees. The same portly Korean steps forward and shrilly proclaims that "God must forgive the archangel Nixon...and bless America!"

The Boston-Sheraton Hotel, November 1978. A gathering of 500 prestigious scientists from around the globe. The conference is chaired by atom bomb scientist and Nobel laureate Eugene Wigner, and is attended by other Nobel prize winners. To loud applause, Dr. Wigner introduces the founder and patron of the annual conference, who rises to address the assembly. It is the same man: Rev. Sun Myung Moon, Lord of the Second Advent, second Adam, One True Parent of the Universe.

As I left for Boonville during our second week in California, I was finally beginning to understand some of the forces behind the smiling faces of the Creative Community Project. I had spent a full day in Daphne Greene's files and briefly interviewed a variety of ex-Moonies; I had learned a lot —though it would be months before a U.S. Congressional Committee studying the Unification Church would release its report, adding valuable pieces to the emerging puzzle of Rev. Moon.

That picture would show that the Creative Community Project, formidable as it looked to us in California, was only a drop in the ocean of Moon's overall activities: a small recruiting arm for a political and industrial empire whose interests dot the globe.

What is this empire? Where did Sun Myung Moon come from, and how did he rise? And what use did his organization have for our friend Benji and thousands like him?

I did not know the answers to all of these questions when I left for Boonville that cloudy fall day—and perhaps it was just as well, since the added knowledge would only have unnerved me more. For apart from Moon's psychological net and his murky political connections—which are separate tales in themselves—his religion is a giant multi-national corporation, whose ultimate goal is to control the world.

Real Estate

No exact figures exist for Rev. Moon's fortune. Sources on the Congressional Committee put it at least $200 million, and possibly as high as a billion dollars. Moon's interests are registered under more than 100 names, in dozens of countries, and their total extent may never be known.

The most visible tip of Moon's financial empire is a real estate industry run by his right-hand man, Col. Bo Hi Pak—a former Korean military attache whom many believe to be the Rasputin behind the smiling Moon. The largest concentration

of Unification Church property is in New York State, where it has played monopoly to the tune of about $30 million. Church purchases in New York City alone have included:
- Manhattan Centre, a former 3000-seat opera house ($2 million).
- The Columbia University Club ($1.2 million).
- The New Yorker Hotel, a 42-storey, 2000-room hotel, ($5.6 million), used as the Church's World Mission Centre.
- The former Tiffany building ($2.4 million).
- A $1.5 million factory complex in Queens and a sprinkling of mansions and property across the city.

Outside New York City, Moon has also bought 410 acres of exclusive Tarrytown, land that is worth over $9 million. The property includes Barrytown, a former Christian Brothers seminary that is now the Church's major east coast "training centre"; another tract intended for a proposed Moon University; and East Garden, formerly the home of the Bronfman family and now the personal residence of Moon himself.

It is here on a sprawling country estate with two pools and a sauna, that the Messiah himself lives in imperial style, with his "holy" wife and nine "sinless" children. Ex-Moonie Judy Stanley lived at East Garden as a baby sitter several years ago; upon arriving, she was handed $16,000 in cash and told to go out and "buy some horses" for the kids.

"I went out shopping with a Japanese Church leader, and we got a black gelding and a few quarterhorses," Judy recalls. "It was amazing...we spent the money as though we were buying toys."

Moon's playthings at East Garden include a 50-foot cabin cruiser that is said to be deliberately two feet longer than that of his neighbor, Laurence Rockefeller. Moon's car is a custom-made Lincoln Continental and his wife's a $20,000 Mercedes Benz, both gifts from members of the Unification Church. His eldest son drove a limousine when Judy Stanley was there; the younger ones tore about the estate on Honda motorcycles.

According to Judy and other ex-Moonies, the property is protected by a patrol of black-belt karate experts who communicate by walkie talkie. Particularly vivid in Judy's memory are the exquisite Korean delicacies that she and other Moonies toiled all day to prepare for Father, sometimes rowing out to the middle of the river to serve him while he fished.

"The dishes were all etched in gold, the glasses were crystal and the cutlery was plated with gold," she says. "We'd stand there in the middle of the river, feeding him delicacies and ginseng wine from one boat to the other, like some kind of ancient galley slaves."

Moon's children are well cared-for too. Several of them attend the exclusive Hackley School, and are somewhat rowdy for "perfect children". Their former babysitter says that they frequently shouted at servants and threw roast beef on the floor if it was not cooked to perfection. The worst was Hyo Jin, 12 at the time, who had a habit of torturing squirrels by tying string to their tails and swinging them around his head. In 1977, he was reportedly expelled from Hackley School for shooting his BB gun at squirrels and the local groundskeeper.

The Church's other major U.S. stronghold is California, where it goes under the name of the Creative Community Project (CCP). Its legal name is New Educational Development Inc. The California wing denied any affiliation with Moon as late as 1975, when a high-level spokesman claimed: "He (Moon) does not even know we exist." The Fraser Committee, however, clearly linked the CCP to Moon's organization.

The California group owns several large tracts of land including the 650-acre Boonville camp, another 300 acres called Camp K, and most recently a $660,000 golf club and resort known as Aetna Springs. They have been trying to open an "education and training seminar" at Aetna Springs since 1976 but were long stymied by a feisty small-town sheriff named Earl Randall, who claimed it would be built "over my dead body."

"They've tried to woo me with cakes, flowers and 'we love you truly' memorabilia. They lied to me and conned me and told me they weren't connected to the Unification Church," said the balding cigar chomping sheriff. "But all they want to do is build another brainwashing centre—and they're not gonna get away with it while I'm around." Randall has since been defeated in his bid for re-election as sheriff.

The California Church also owns a gamut of sprawling manors across San Francisco, including William Randolph Hearst's mansion. Many of these houses are accorded tax-exempt status as religious institutions, though critics of the Church have managed to get others back on the tax rolls.

The Ponderosa of the West Coast family is West Eden, the $325,000 home of Mose (Martin) Durst, director of the West Coast Creative Community Project. Durst is an English professor at Laney College and joined the Church's hierarchy after marrying Moon missionary Ooni Kim. Ex-Moonies who have visited the couple's residence describe a magnificent manor with a park, an enclosed pool and a sauna. Four Church members act as servants, closets are stuffed with furs and silk dressing gowns, and a solid-gold replica of a Korean crown is said to adorn the living room.

Moon homes, centres and estates also dot other parts of the U.S., ranging from the $50,000 Windermere House in Seattle to a $500,000 home in Boston, and the Church continues to add to its property. In Canada, similar homes are springing up in several major cities, varying from a $100,000 home in Montreal to a more elaborate home in Toronto, priced at over $300,000. They also own a 95-acre estate in Rice Lake, Ontario, which was the residence of former Governor-General Georges Vanier.

Moon's overall plans for the future are even more ambitious. He has instructed members to work so hard they bring in $30 million a month.

"Then we can buy Pan American Airlines...the Ford Motor Company...not to mention the Empire State Building."

Business Ventures

The money to finance these Church estates comes from amoeba-like business ventures flung out across the world. In Canada, Moonies sell cosmetics and candy door-to-door, in France they run a successful jewellery business, in England they publish a daily newspaper, and in Japan they own a variety of small manufacturing firms.

The stronghold of Moon's empire is Korea, where five companies churn out everthing from textiles and marble vases to ginseng tea and sophisticated machine tools. The most controversial of the Messiah's Korean holding is a major weapons plant that was unearthed by the Fraser Committee. According to the committee, Moon's Tong-Il Industries is the chief weapons supplier for Korea, producing M-16 rifles, vulcan anti-aircraft guns and M-79 grenade launchers—peculiar products for a "Messiah of Peace".

Moon's Korean businesses are said to be worth some $15 million on paper but Congressional sources estimate that his secret weapons contract and world-wide success in marketing ginseng tea boost the value of his Korean investments to nearly $100 million. All Korean businesses are run by members of the Unification Church, who receive no or low wages and work long, unregulated hours. However, Moon has no labor problems; as Col. Bo Hi Pak explained to West coast journalist Andrew Ross:

"Rev. Moon has a different kind of management...the workers are happy to serve God and the Unification Church."

Even Moon's Korean investments are beginning to pale in comparison to the growing diversity of his U.S. empire—a decentralized network of enterprises that range from multimillion dollar corporations to tiny community stores. There are travel agencies, restaurants, printing firms, tea shops, cleaning companies and consulting firms; no sooner does one close down than others spring up—often under elaborate corporate names such as "The Centre for Ethical Management (CEMP) or the New Hope Singers International.

There are also a variety of organizations whose sole purpose is to attract new members, often without revealing their links to the Unification Church. The Creative Community Project is one example, others are the Collegiate Association for the Research of Principles (CARP), the Church's main recruiting wing on U.S. college campuses, and HARP, its high school wing. All told, Moon enterprises have operated under at least 50 names in the U.S., often in clandestine and probably illegal fashion. The Fraser Committee found evidence that Moon had "systematically violated" U.S. tax, immigration, currency, banking and other laws; they recommended setting up an inter-agency task force to investigate Moon's empire further. A summary of some of Moon's more interesting U.S. businesses follows:

International Press and Exchange Maintenance [IPEM]

IPEM, a potpourri of services operated by the western division of the Unification Church, work, for both government and private companies. They have won contracts to clean carpets in several U.S. federal buildings, including Air Force bases and the FBI offices in Sacramento; they also printed bus tokens for the San Francisco Municipal Railway.

They have done maintenance work for the Playboy Club, the Hyatt Regency Hotel and Best Western Hotels. They report to work promptly, crisply dressed in shirts and ties. This seems to impress their customers: their ads display a letter from a top official of Holiday Inn thanking them for their "high standards...fair prices...and over-all enthusiasm".

Aladdin's

Another West Coast venture, this popular restaurant bordering Berkeley is an excellent example of the way Moonie enterprises blend like chameleons into the communities they serve. Waterfalls gurgle down the restaurant walls, Moonie waiters flash perpetual smiles and a well-stocked bar buttresses the menu, despite the Church's abhorrence of liquor.

"Welcome to the best Kosher restaurant in San Francisco" says the sign on the door. "The best Jewish deli in the West," announces another, offering "real bagels, chopped liver, gefilte fish, blintzes, knishes, borscht, Jewish pickles and cheese cake like Lindy's. Also serves weddings and Bar Mitzvahs."

The spiel is effective. The restaurant is packed at lunchtime and recently expanded. Customers down smoked meat and cold beer, oblivious to the restaurant's ownership; those who know about it ask: "Why shouldn't the Moonies make a buck too?"

The answer is behind the scenes. Jeff Scales, a former Moonie who managed Aladdin's for more than a year, has testified that the entire staff worked 80 hours a week; Scales himself worked more than a 110 hour week. Although the restaurant took in between $3000 and $4000 a week, according to Scales, all paychecks were signed back to the "management".

News World

Moon's daily New York City newspaper lost between five and ten million dollars in its first two years of operation, but began to turn the corner during the 1978 New York newspaper strike. While employees at all the major papers walked off the job, the non-unionized Moonie paper boosted its circulation from 30,000 to 400,000, making News World the most widely read paper in New York City. According to the paper's officials, circulation has levelled off at about 87,000 since the strike, but critics say it is no higher than 50,000.

The paper claims to be independent of the Church, but it consistently plugs Moon-related activities and attacks his enemies. It printed an article accusing Rep. Donald Fraser head of the committee investigating the Moonies, of being a "communist agent".

Until 1978, the paper relied on a staff of some 150 Church members. But then, in a move that could hint at Moon's overall business strategy for the future, the paper hired six veteran newsmen to improve its image. Among them was Harry J. Staphos, a roly-poly newsman who had been slogging behind the scenes at the New York Daily News for more than ten years; the Moonies offered to put Staphos' byline on page one, and he leapt at the chance.

"Look, at the News I was on rewrite desk for life...but here I write my own ticket," says Staphos candidly. "I do page one features all the time."

While Moonie staff members receive no pay and eat peanut butter sandwiches every lunchtime, Staphos is well paid. "They asked me how much it would take to get me...I rattled off some crazy figures...and they said 'sure'.

"But I figure I'm worth the price. Before I came, they didn't get invited to anything...they were persona non grata. But since I joined, they get invited to everything...and all kinds of people are reading their paper. Now they're legit."

The Church has other footholds in the media. They run a daily Paper in Tokyo called the *Sekai Nippo,* and have started another in London. In Washington, Church members distribute *The Rising Tide,* a glossy weekly newsletter delivered free to every congress member and aide on Capitol Hill; in Canada, they sell *Our Canada,* purportedly the organ of a group called Canadian Unity Freedom Foundation—in reality, another Moon front.

As well, the Church turns out hundreds of slick one-shot newspapers, magazines and newsletters with names like *Good News,* aimed at everyone from grade school and high school children to Jewish groups and immigrants.

Recently, the Church moved into the film business, founding a company called One Way Productions, with offices in Tokyo and Los Angeles. They turn out Moon-related PR documentaries and have reportedly invested 18 million dollars in "Oh Inchon"—Robin Moore's tale of General MacArthur's landing in Korea.

Fishing

One of the Church's latest and most serious enterprises is the fishing industry, where Moon is said to be prepared to spend $25 million. Typical of the Church's approach was its entry into the sleepy, fishing village of Bayou La Battree, Louisiana, a town with a population of 2500 and a long history of fishing tied up in legendary shrimpers such as Clam Pie Annie and French Evelyn.

In 1977, a company called International Seafood swept into town, buying up some $6 million of boat-building businesses and choice waterfront land. Local snooping soon revealed that the company was owned by a parent group called International Oceanic Enterprises, which in turn was entirely controlled by the Unification Church.

A local group, Concerned Citizens of the South, has since formed to try to limit the Moonies' presence in Bayou. But local small fishermen still watch the launching of huge tuna boats into their waters and worry that with a combination of capital, long working hours and free labour, the Moonies may eventually put them out of business. Others worry about the Moonies potential effect on the town's young people, and even about the possibility that they will eventually control the town—which has only 750 registered voters.

In the meantime, the Church has spread its tentacles into other fishing towns as well. They have invested more than a million dollars in Norfolk, Virginia; spent $300,000 on a lobster packing plant in Gloucester, Massachusetts; launched boats in Long Island, New York, and recently announced the acquisition of a $3 million shrimp business in Kodiak, Alaska.

Church officials maintain that their fishing business is just part of their "spiritual activities", because fishing is "a great test of the mind" and also a "religious experience" symbolic of fishing for the souls of men.

Diplomat National Bank

For a brief period in 1976, the Moon empire virtually controlled an American Bank, the Diplomat National based in

Washington. Federal laws prevented anyone (or any group) from owning more than five per cent of a U.S. bank's capital, but the Fraser Committee found that Moon and his associates disguised the source of their funds to try to take control of the bank.

The Fraser Committee said more than 53% of the bank's capital was secretly held by persons affiliated with the Moon organization. The Committee concluded that the Church had tried to take control of the bank in order to move large amounts of money between Moon businesses and the countries in which they operated, without arousing the attention of neutral bank officials.

The Unification Church had the largest account in the Diplomat Bank, under the name United Church International; between late 1975 and early 1976, this account served as a clearinghouse for more than $7 million, quietly dispatched by Moon and Bo Hi Pak to a wide variety of church-related businesses and personal accounts.

Adverse newspaper publicity in the spring of 1976, interrupted the operation, and federal authorities soon forced Church members to divest their shares.

Flower-Selling

Remarkably, despite so many business ventures, the backbone of the Church's cash flow has always been selling flowers on the street. Flower-peddling combines Moonie zeal with deceptive sales practices, referred to as "heavenly deception", to bring in between $20 million and $50 million a year, according to former members.

From Flin Flon, Canada to the Florida Keys, troops of Moonies move about in Mobile Fundraising Teams (MFT), fervently button-holing customers in the streets of tiny towns and major cities. They frequently misrepresent themselves; ex-members have said that members routinely claimed to work for ghetto children, California migrant farm workers the B'nai Brith and dozens of other causes.

"Our bar sales would be flowers that were dead two days before," writes ex-flower team leader Barbara Underwood.

"We'd just wrap them up in green paper to disguise them. I made as much as $400 a day regularly, but I never felt I was doing enough."

MFT is the most gruelling of all Moonie activities. Members sleep and eat little, and spend their nights driving to new towns or packaging flowers for the next day's sales. "People would see us at 9 a.m., then they'd pass us at 6 p.m. and again at midnight—and they'd be impressed," recalls one former Moonie who peddled flowers in northern Canada. "They'd say 'poor kid'—and buy our flowers to help us out."

Most Moonies bring in at least $100 a day, but figures as high as $400 are not uncommon. Females often do better; in Canada, two-person female teams have regularly brought in more than a $1000 a day. Recently, however, publicity in the news media has caught up with the flower-selling and reportedly hurt sales badly.

The flower-selling enterprise exemplifies the advantages the Unification Church gets from mixing religion and business. The money collected from church-related activities such as flower-selling is tax-exempt and the total proceeds are unaccountable and unknown.

Yet the Fraser Committee found that the pool of tax-free money was often used to help out Moon business interests that have nothing to do with the religious aspects of the Moon organization. For instance, when *New World* began, some $2 million in tax-free funds was lent to the paper by the Church to help keep it afloat—an enormous advantage that secular businesses do not have.

An even more important advantage in mixing business and religion into the same "family" is ready cheap labor. At the base of all Moon businesses is the tireless labor of the Moonies—dedicated "missionaries" who work as many as 22 hours a day for no pay and little food to bring in money for God.

Convinced that the Church hovers perpetually on the brink of bankruptcy, and that the money they earn is indispensable to building a "foundation" for a "better world", they labor ceaselessly at all Moon enterprises: they have no unions, no regular hours and no rights, and they usually sign their paychecks back to the Church.

For their efforts, members receive meagre material returns: a piece of floor in a Moonie house, some second-hand clothes, a "heavenly haircut" and a diet ranging from vegetable stew at "home" to occasional MacDonald burgers on the road. Many of the Moon-related businesses run 24 hours a day, enabling them to provide quick, cheap service that draws rave notices from customers.

"With no labor costs and people willing to work 15 hours a day, you can undercut anyone," says Jeff Scales, former manager of Aladdin's. Scales says he once took about $20,000 from staff's salaries to buy a metallic blue Mercedes as a gift for California leaders Mose and Ooni Durst.

"You must not sleep much, eat much, rest much," Moon tells his members. "You must work day and night to make this great task a reality. You must move on right to the moment of death...eating, sleeping, resting...these are of no concern to me."

Moon also tells members that they must resist "sleepy spirits", and he boasts of driving across America at "115 miles an hour" with no sleep. It is not surprising that many ex-members report frequent and serious car accidents.

"We were in a lot of car accidents because people were so tired," reports ex-Moonie Barbara Underwood. "Our car was totalled once. Another car had the front smashed in. They were always because somebody fell asleep."

Disease is similarly regarded as a "weakness" to be overcome by mental discipline; many Moonies have been told to leave injuries, rashes and illnesses untreated because Satan was acting through them and had to be "fought off." Even eating is viewed as a weakness that can be overcome; fasts are frequent despite the length of the working day. This gruelling lifestyle can have powerful effects on the psychological state of converts; one ex-member, Leslie Brown, recalled this experience she had while fund-raising:

"I had made a goal not to eat anything that day, but I had a good day (several hundred dollars) and someone offered me a little piece of chocolate which I ate...my legs became lead. I couldn't speak to people. I was frozen in misery for 45 minutes...and as my whole body trembled—I still don't believe it—a deep man's voice came rumbling out of me and said:

'LESLIE! You've made a base agreement with *Satan*. You can't work with God *anymore.*' "

Sun Myung Moon

The Messiah who wields this remarkable power is a 60 year old Korean with a taste for blue business suits and disco shirts, and a speaking style known to drive casual spectators from the hall in droves. There is no evidence that he was ever ordained a minister.

The chunky evangelist first broke into the North American scene in 1971, when posters of his smiling face festooned drugstores, subways and newspapers across New York —heralding his arrival and inviting members of the public to their "re-birthday." It was the start of a three-year cross country blitz touching every major city in the U.S., providing lavish dinners for thousands of prominent people in churches, business and politics and thrusting Moon into the headlines time and again. Yet despite his sudden appearance in the North American limelight, the making of the moneyed Messiah had begun many years before.

Moon was born into a struggling Presbyterian family on January 6, 1920 in a tiny village that is now part of North Korea. His name at birth was Yong Myung Moon, "Shining Sun Dragon"; when he began preaching in 1946 he changed it to the more imposing Sun Myung Moon, "Shining Sun and Moon".

Information on his childhood is sparse, although a Unification Church historian has him tracking weasels "across snow-covered Korean mountains all night long," and catching "slippery eels with bare hands" by day. His parents were poor farmers, but put him through high school and later Waseda University, where his interests were electricity and wrestling; in fact, he might have gone on to become an innocuous electrician but for the events of Easter Sunday, 1936.

According to Moon, he was deep in prayer on a mountaintop that day, when a blinding vision of Christ appeared and a powerful voice rumbled from the heavens: "I am Jesus who came 2000 years ago. Now you will complete what I began but was unable to finish."

In the wake of this experience, Moon began to travel and gather a flock. During these early years he was married at least twice, and managed to get himself excommunicated from the Presbyterian Church and refused entry by the Korean National Council of Churches.

He was also arrested on several occasions for reasons that are disputed. Moon says it was for his anti-communism; other information, including Korean newspaper accounts of the time, suggest it may have been for peculiar sex practices.

In fact, Moon first came to prominence in Korea in 1955 when a scandal broke out at fashionable Ewha Women's College over several girls and prominent female professors said to be involved in the "scandalous rites of the Unification Church." Don Ranard, a top official for the U.S. State Department in Korea in the late 1950's, says CIA files at the time were full of sexual allegations about Moon. "We were getting reports, calls and letters alleging that the Unification Church was a sexually-oriented mixing of people in orgy-type fashion, in which Moon was the tester of virginity for new members," Ranard said in a telephone interview. Moon denies this.

"This was one of the first things that aroused our attention to him...he seemed to be a real Oriental Elmer Gantry."

In 1947 Moon was imprisoned by the Communists and spent three years in Hungnam Prison, until General MacArthur freed him in 1950—only hours before his execution, if one believes Church literature. The Church plays Moon's entire ordeal to the hilt; it claims that at one point he lost so much blood that members thought he was dead and "began funeral preparations, but within three days he mysteriously revived—and although the blood was almost drained from his body...he immediately rose and began to preach out his powerful message, the Divine Principle."

The Divine Principle. This is the theology that lies at the root of the Moonie philosophy: a complicated mixture of Taoism, Buddhism, Confucianism, fetishism, some Christianity, and traces of electrical engineering—all bound into a 536-page black book that resembles a Bible.

At the core of this theology is Moon's interpretation of the "Fall of Man." According to Moon, Adam and Eve were born sinless and meant to live in the Garden of Eden but Satan seduced Eve sexually and tainted her blood forever. Instead of confessing her crime, Eve then aggravated matters by having sex with Adam and bearing children.

Consequently, their descendants—the entire human race—are "fallen", their bloodline poisoned by Satan for all time; thus nothing that a human being does—regardless of how well-intentioned, can possibly escape its evil roots. According to Moon, the arrival of Jesus gave man a second chance—but Jesus neglected to complete his mission; he failed to marry and have "pure" children, and before he could correct this oversight Satan acted through the Jews to kill him.

Moon's Divine Principle says that a third Adam, the Lord of the Second Advent, will come from the East sometime in the 1920's (the time of Moon's own birth), and work to restore mankind. If all goes well, he will correct the state of the world, then marry and father "sinless children" who, along with Moon's followers, will form a vanguard force to eliminate Satan and restore Heaven—not in some cloudy afterworld, but right here on earth.

This is the key to the behavior of the fully-indoctrinated Moonie. He believes that he is involved in a cataclysmic battle between the omnipresent forces of Evil and the tiny vanguard of Good; failure to succeed may mean the rule of Satan for thousands of years more, with nuclear obliteration likely to finish us off before we get another chance to correct things. This is why Moonies must work tirelessly, and why they must swear off "tainted sex" until Moon declares that they have become "sinless".

At that point he chooses a mate for them and marries them off in mass weddings that he holds every few years. Moon married 1800 couples in Seoul in 1975; he is currently planning another giant affair for Boston sometime in 1980. He has alrady matched up 701 couples in expectation, many to mates they have never met.

Divine Principle does not explicitly state that Moon is the Messiah, but it is an implicit truth for most longtime members. It is also accepted gospel that South Korea (Moon's home) must be preserved at all costs—a belief that dovetails with the Church's anti-communist, pro-South Korea political line. Following this logic, Satan's main earthly face is communism, the anti-Christ; so Moon and his members must devote all their time and energy to battling the communist "devil" around the world. Many ex-members have said that they were prepared to die for Korea, and Moon suggested as much himself in a speech in Seoul in 1975:

> "It is the world members of the Unification Church who believe Korea is their religious Fatherland and their holy land. For a faithful religious person, to invade this holy land is to invade his own body and home. This means that the world members of the Unification Church love Korea as their own physical bodies...*they believe it is God's will to protect their religious Fatherland to the last, to organize the Unification Crusade Army and to take part in the world as a supporting force to defend both Korea and the free world.*"

Armed with his rather tortuous philosophy, Moon and a few disciples founded the Unification Church in 1954 under what is still its official name: the Holy Spirit Association for the Unification of World Christianity. But neither the movement nor its Messiah got very far until 1960-61, vintage years for Moon and his church.

First Moon married again, this time the ravishing eighteen-year-old Hak-Ja Han, who became "Mother of the Universe" and bore him the first of eleven "sinless children". More importantly, May of 1961 saw a revolt by South Korea's colonels—a political upheaval that altered the future of that country and the Moon Church.

The man who took control of South Korea was Col. Park Chung Hee, a ruthless dictator who curtailed democracy and suppressed every Christian religion in Korea except one—the Unification Church. In 1961, Moon's Church claimed 32,000 members in Korea; by 1969 the figure reached 300,000. The Church now claims a half-million members world-wide; critics say there are no more than 200,000.

The U.S. branch of the Church began officially in 1961, when Col. Bo Hi Pak and a handful of Koreans set up a small organization with a membership mainly limited to religious eccentrics; it was this group that served as a base for Moon when he began his blitz of the U.S. in 1971.

There are many questions about where Moon obtained the approximately $8 million needed to finance his early American tours, since he was not personally wealthy at the time, and the Church's American membership was far too small and impoverished to fund him. Observers speculate that the money came from either the Korean Government, or wealthy right-wing industrialists in Japan.

In any case, when Moon arrived in 1971, he furiously reorganized the U.S. Church, changing its structures and beginning a major recruiting drive. According to Gary Scharff, a top Moon instructor at the time, Moon singlehandedly brought in the rigid indoctrination techniques that were first practised at the New York Barrytown centre under the title of "100-day Training Program".

"Moon gave us the specifics as soon as he arrived from Korea," recalls Scharff. "The hours a day, the precision of activities, the discipline—we had to be up at 6 a.m. and in formation at 6:08 like the cadets. Moon developed the 100-day training program entirely on his own...he's a very effective human manipulator."

Moon's heavy-handed methods were immediately effective at turning veteran Church members into disciplined zealots, but did not attract youth of the sixties generation. The Church required one more addition before it could begin its ascendancy in America: the arrival of Dr. Mose Durst, a west coast English teacher who coated Moon's mind-bending indoctrination techniques with the sophisticated honey of 1960's counterculture jargon.

Durst, a fuzzy-haired faculty member at California's Laney College, married Church missionary Ooni Kim, and became head of the Western organization. He soon helped introduce many of the features of today's Boonville program: the deception, misrepresentation and progressive indoctrination that lures recruits into the Church step by step. Later they are often sent to complete their training at New York's more military 100-day program.

Boonville quickly became the most effective recruiting centre for the Church; for the first time, the Moonies began to attract large numbers of articulate, formerly stable college kids with no easily detectable personal problems. Other centres began to emulate Boonville's approach, and by 1977 the Church claimed some 32,000 North American members —though critics say that figure was exaggerated.

There is no information on what percentage of the Church's membership comes in through the Boonville port of entry; but it is unquestionably their most successful recruiting centre, responsible for as much as two-thirds of the Church's overall North American recruiting.

The Eastern branch of the Church runs most of Moon's major business and public relations activity, but it is more straightforward (and less successful) in its recruitment approach. It periodically denounces the deception and trickery of its Western wing, just as Church officials deny any connection with many of its other financial and political subsidiaries. The easterners claim Boonville graduates are deprogrammed more easily and make less effective members; there are even rumors about an imminent split between the two branches.

But the fact remains that without the techniques introduced in California, the Church's membership would never have soared; simply put, the Unification Church, as it is known today, would not exist. The Boonville experience lies at the heart of the Church's power.

4

A seemingly endless gravel road halted abruptly at a high barbed-wire fence and a wooden sentry post. It was midnight, the end of a three-hour van ride from San Francisco, as headlights pierced the blackness, illuminating a sign reading "Boonville Ideal City Ranch."

My stomach grew queasy. Everything I had heard about Boonville made me apprehensive, particularly the many stories of people whose personalities had changed here in only a few days. Even one graduate student studying the camp for academic purposes had succumbed, and the only reporter whose firsthand account I had read had collapsed vomiting and hallucinating on fleeing the camp after 48 hours.

I was so nervous I had left a signed statement with Marilyn asking her to retrieve me legally if I would not leave on my own, and my apprehension had increased when the Moonies required me to sign a form before leaving Washington House "releasing CCP project from all responsibility and liability in the seminar experience."

Now as I stepped out of the van and padded through the wet grass, a light mist further cloaked the darkness, making vision nearly impossible. We were herded toward a shadowy metal structure and urged to bed down immediately.

"I'm gonna grab a cigarette outside," mumbled one recruit, the spitting image of a young Jack Nicholson.

"Sorry. We prefer you don't smoke," replied a Moonie

male, as he firmly motioned the newcomer toward the sleeping quarters. "Also we'd appreciate if you'd hit the sack right away. Tomorrow's going to be a long, tiring day."

Inside the barn-like structure, scraps of thin foam and a wooden floor awaited. Bodies were sprawled everywhere, lit by a dim lamp outside. A gentle rain was beginning to fall on the tin roof and the wind howled in the distance.

I curled up in the corner beside Jack Nicholson: he seemed an amiable fellow, and as the lights went out he whistled softly into the pitch dark and whispered a single word:

"Bi-zarrrre!"

The night's drizzle was just waning when I was roused from restless sleep by a chorus of robust voices: they were singing "Raindrops Keep Falling on my Head."

In seconds, bodies were leaping into their clothes and exuberant hands were hauling me from bed, into a circle of people gathering to sing wake-up songs.

"Good morning everyone!" boomed a clean-cut guitar player wearing a v-neck sweater and a wide toothpaste commercial smile. "How are *you?*"

"Ter-r-r-rific!" thundered dozens of smiling faces. Then my hands were clasped and the entire group burst into a 30-minute session of cheery tunes. It was seven a.m. on a wet Tuesday morning, and as I squinted through tired eyes, life at Boonville was roaring into gear.

Tucked into the gentle rolling forest of Mendocino County, some 120 miles north of San Francisco, the 650-acre camp was a large, pleasant site with simple accommodations. Long grassy field stretched from the main compound, consisting of a clump of trailers and a small home-made hanging bridge.

In the distance, the forest stood against a flat, grey horizon; an eight-foot barbed-wire fence circled the entire farm. Still, standing in the country air that morning, surrounded by warm, wholesome faces and vibrant singing, my original paranoia seemed far away and unfounded. The Moonies looked like friendly people—a bit straight perhaps, but tales of the camp seemed at least exaggerated.

The building we had slept in was a huge converted chicken coop affectionately dubbed the "Chicken Palace". Women slept separately in a nearby trailer.

Bathrooms were modest wooden cabins labelled "brothers" and "sisters," stocked with drugstore shelves of everything from shaving cream and dental floss to rows of collective toothbrushes. Inside a row of Moonies were busily applying razor blades to their fresh pink cheeks.

"Like to shave?" asked one, motioning toward my fuzzy beard. I quickly declined. Minutes later, another young Moonie took my hand and escorted me back to the Chicken Palace, where exercise period had just begun.

This lasted some 45 minutes, mixing stride jumps and jumping jacks with "wiggling our toenails" and "balancing elephants on our shoulders". All activity was punctuated by endless clapping and cheering, particularly the "family cheer", a seemingly innocent little chant called a "chooch" that required us to link arms and holler:

"*Ch-ch-choo, ch-ch-choo, ch-ch-choo. Yea! Yea! POW!!*"

Most recruits appeared to find the chooch a little silly, but went along with it out of politeness; it seemed rude to decline. Most of the recruits during my stay were male—a fairly normal-looking lot, easily distinguished from their Moonie hosts by their unkempt hair and scraggly looks. My own favourite was Keith, the "mountain man"—a sort of hippie Paul Bunyan to whom I took an instant liking. He said he came from a small Carolina town called "Loafers Glory", wore a battered old stetson and had little to say to the yattering of the Moonies but "yup" and "nope".

By now, each recruit had attracted a family member of the opposite sex, who encouraged us to participate. Mine was Bethie, who said she had promised Benji she'd be "adopting" me.

Unrelenting activity, enthusiastic chatter and hand-holding soon proved to be the most notable features of life with the Moonies. I was asked dozens of personal questions about myself and my friendship with Benji and prodded to sing and cheer continuously. When breakfast finally arrived 90 minutes after wake-up, I was as eager for a breather and some personal space as I was for the apple stew and coffee that was served. But meals, I soon found, were another link in a chain of totally structured activity that continued unbroken until day's end.

"We have a custom during meals," explained the ever-exuberant Bethie, our group leader. "We like to *share* something with each other. You know...just a little tidbit to help us get to know one another."

"Sharing" required each person to divulge a bit about his or her life story and innermost feelings. It began gently enough during breakfast with small personal resumes, but as the day went on sharing became a virtual encounter session, with emotional confessions about everything from "selfishness" to former sexual activity. New recruits participated too, moved by the honesty of others. Under the circumstances it seemed uptight, even rude, not to offer a "bit of yourself".

Fortunately, I had already learned from ex-Moonies that group leaders discussed our confessions in private, using them to zero in on our psychological weak spots and potential guilt feelings.

I gave my own prepared story, sticking fairly close to the truth because I knew Benji might have briefed them; however, sensing that doubt was valued, I added that I was on sabbatical to "appraise things". I was beginning to have doubts about my "identity" as a journalist. After my confession, and each of the others, the Moonies politely applauded.

During the meal my food was seasoned, my coffee doused with cream and everything done for me but the positioning of the fork in my mouth. I found myself repeating the word "thanks" with monotonous regularity, and hating the increased sense of obligation to participate that came with it.

As well, my hands were being held and fondled as though

they were communal property.

"It's hard to be an unselfish person, to start thinking about the good of others before you think of yourself," Bethie told the neat rows of "students" assembled at our first "lecture". She stood at the blackboard for more than an hour, and the word "selfish" was repeated more than thirty times.

"It's hard to sing when others feel like singing, or to hold someone's clammy hand, just because they want you to," she said with an understanding smile, as though reading our thoughts. "Nowadays people are used to doing their own thing."

Like Kristina's lecture at the house the talk was presented as a spontaneous "rap", yet struck me as being meticulously prepared, weaving history, science, philosophy and psychology into a compelling appeal to build a "better world."

It was absorbing, humorous, thought-provoking and confusing: ideas wheeled by like railway cars on a speeding train; far too quickly to examine critically. If my eyes wandered for even an instant, a helpful family member would prod me politely and say:

"Josh, try to listen. This part is *very* important." It was not until the second day that I noticed a subtle but continual jockeying of seats to make sure that I and other recruits were always surrounded by such mindful family members.

Feelings were weak and intellectual discipline strong, we were told during that first lecture: we were to try and adapt to what at first seemed a weird and trying experience. Also we were asked to stay completely away from other new recruits, so as not to reinforce each other's "negativity".

"We're trying to set up a model community here in Boonville, where people act according to their ideals, not just their feelings," the lecture concluded. "It takes discipline at first, but try and see it as a two-day experiment in a different way of living, no matter how silly and foreign it may sometimes seem. Be *strong*—don't just give up and head home...*please.*"

She need hardly have asked. We were 120 miles in the middle of who-knew-where, and they owned the only vehicle.

After each lecture, we met in small groups to discuss our reactions, but critical questions were skillfully circumvented by the leaders or simply put off with "Let's not get hung up on that now. The lectures will deal with that later." They never did.

Seconds later we would be lost in another dizzying stream of singing, hand-holding and the inevitable chooch:

"Ch-ch-choo, ch-ch-choo, ch-ch-choo. Yea! Yea! POW!!"

It was exhausting. My mind swam from ceaseless noise and activity, and there was never time to reflect or even daydream without someone immediately asking me what I was thinking about. Time began to stretch and distort like liquid oozing from a bottle, and I longed for a watch to see if it was ten o'clock or two.

"Coffee break!" announced Bethie suddenly, and I scrambled to my feet and headed outside for respite. I hadn't taken three steps when a clammy hand came down on my shoulder and a voice asked: "So how do you like it so far, Josh?"

Turning I found myself inches from the flaccid face of Jim, a chubby fellow with Coke-bottle-bottom glasses and a limp smile common to many male Moonies—a dull, hollow look in the midst of apparent enthusiasm that reminds one of the androids that fetch Boris Karloff's coffee in late-night horror movies.

"Well...uh...actually..." I stammered. "I haven't really had time to think about it much yet...let me think on it some and I'll talk to you about it later."

"But Josh, what parts of the lecture did you want to think about?" he persevered.

"Look," I said. "I'm sorry, but I need a bit of time to collect my thoughts. I'm going to take a quick walk."

"Great!" he said, staring at me even more intently, with another disembodied smile, as he threw an arm around me.

"I'll come along too."

I paused to collect my thoughts. I felt guilty at the thought of rejecting him again, but I knew I needed a moment alone. I stared at Jim as intently as I could, meeting his unnerving gaze head on.

"No!", I declared, then turned and walked quickly away. I am an extrovert and do not ordinarily need much time alone, but I floated in those few seconds of solitude as though I had been released from a crippling weight. Seconds later, two women came rushing over bubbling "Josh! Josh! Josh!" as though I were a boyfriend they hadn't seen in years.

"Boy Josh, you sure are an interesting character," giggled one of them as she and her friend fished my unwilling hands from my pockets and fondled them. Minutes later, after a quick stop for two cups of black coffee, I was back in the lecture room again.

"They said Columbus was crazy—but 50 years later there was a settlement in North America," explained Bethie, as several family members leapt up in seemingly spontaneous guerrilla theatre shouting: "You're crazy Columbus—you're nuts."

"They said Orville Wright was crazy too—even his own mother thought he was weird—but today man has walked on the moon! So why is the idea of building an ideal world so crazy...today?"

Ideas were repeated in a variety of ways, hammering the message home with hypnotic effect, while skits and humour kept the atmosphere light. "Skepticism is negativity", was the growing message, and negativity is what puts "a ceiling on our happiness and holds us back."

"Remember those really special moments, those points of ecstasy...well, those are portholes into what happiness really is. At maturity you will feel that way all the time—no insecurities, no worries."

It was a hip sermon. Doom and gloom statistics chugged forth like black smoke from a locomotive: 1.6 million kids run away every year, 1 in 100 of them is killed, 1 in 80 beaten;

everyone is insecure and worried about their image; TV, promiscuity and drugs threaten the world; communism is a good idea turned horribly sour.
"It's easy to pay $1000 to hear 'I'm O.K., you're O.K.' Here you pay $18 to hear you're selfish and greedy."
Toynbee, Spengler, Einstein and Maslow; Mao, Buddha and Confucious were all invoked at one point or another, losing me in a haze of names and data. Much of the information seemed to be a logical outgrowth of concepts from the earlier lecture, but I still hadn't absorbed that information and I found myself getting lost, mentally seasick in a churning flood of new ideas. Yet, no sooner did my eyes wander than a friendly poke would invoke my "discipline" again.
Nothing quite seemed to make sense anymore. All I knew for sure was that there still was not the slightest mention of the most important element of the group's philosophy—the Reverend Sun Myung Moon.

By 3 o'clock of the same day I was worried. The ceaseless chanting and singing was echoing in my ears, the chooch as grating as a nail dragged across a blackboard. The sharing sessions were uncomfortably intimate. Even the handholding had become unbearable: some hands were sticky, some flaccid, some like sandpaper; others that fondled and squeezed me felt more like snakes than human beings.
The camp was proving a strange mix of boot camp, kindergarten and psychotherapy session, and it was getting to me. Some of the other recruits seemed at least as uncomfortable as I, but since they didn't know what the group was or what they were up to, they blamed themselves for being too egotistic and tried harder to participate. The silence between new recruits was a blanket that muffled dissent and prevented people from comparing notes and reinforcing their doubts. Everyone was locked inside his own world, convinced he was the lone dissenter yet less and less sure he was right to dissent.
Some recruits were already caught up completely, ab-

sorbed by what seemed a remarkably sincere and idealistic, if odd experience. Only my original cynicism kept me consciously resisting, and even that was barely enough to get me through the afternoon's "kickball game".

The ride to the athletic field was pleasant enough, the rumble of the pick-up truck allowing me to steal a few moments of conversation with Keith, the mountain man. Tales of Loafers Glory; the annual Bug Frying Contest, the arm wrestling matches and the Loafers Glory Spud Eating Marathon gave me my first light moments on the farm. Keith had spent five years in the backwoods, "thinkin' and drinkin'," and six unfortunate months in jail for moonshining; he could guarantee that his cell had been exactly 144 bricks long, 42 bricks wide and held together by 114 rivets.

"Wow...what a beautiful sunset!" broke in the loud, flat voice of a Moonie as he pointed west, and every head in the truck turned to watch. "Everyone look at the beautiful sunset."

"Wow!" went forty voices, as one.

From the instant we arrived at the kickball field for what had been billed as our afternoon "break", we began singing and cheering wildly, as teams were somehow arranged.

Arms drew me into a huddle, where our team captain Muffy interrupted the cheering to give an impassioned "pep talk."

"We're gonna beat them...we're gonna beat them so bad they're not gonna believe what hit them!" she enthused. "And why?"

"Because we LOVE them!"

"*Ya-aa-aayyyy!*"

Then a cheer began: "BOOT WITH LOVE! BOOT WITH LOVE! BOOT WITH LOVE!" The maddening refrain was repeated over and over without a second's pause. Veteran Moonies exhorted recruits to keep up with the avalanche of noise: "BOOTWITHLOVE! BOOTWITHLOVE! BOOTWITHLOVE!"

"CATCH WITH LOVE! CATCH WITH LOVE! CATCH

WITH LOVE!'' shrieked the other team as the two cheers drowned each other into meaningless, deafening sound.

The chanting continued hypnotically, without let-up for two hours. It did not rise or fall with good or bad plays: it simply continued, like a television set accidentally left on at maximum volume.

"BOOTWITHLOVE! CATCHWITHLOVE! BOOTWITH-LOVE!"

I lost my voice in fifteen minutes, but was cajoled into mouthing the words far longer. Other recruits chanted limply "Boot---Catch---Boot" trying to keep up. Comparisons with experiences like summer camp were futile. I spent much of my early life in camps, and the cheers during excited moments of play there have as much to do with the barrage of noise at Boonville as a playground resembles a battlefield. The experience was so disorienting that at times it seemed to me the field tilted in space, as though I were on board a plane.

As with so many other techniques at Boonville, the purpose of the mind-numbing chant was to keep us from "spacing out", from finding seconds to daydream and possibly entertain "negative" or unproductive thoughts about life at the camp. For the same reason, when our bus lurched into the mud on the ride back from the game we did not stop to push it out, but filed off quickly, back to the routine of the camp, leaving the group leaders to solve the problem.

"I used to hate the noise at the kickball game," one novice Moonie named Geno explained to me, as he tried to sell me on the virtues of the chant. "I used to hate everything about it. But now I see where its helped me very much. I hardly ever space out any more, not even for a second, and that means I can give one hundred per cent to the project, all the time...I've even learned to *like* the noise."

Fortunately, an unplanned moment of relief from "one hundred per cent" was provided me halfway through the kickball game, when I got a base hit. As I rounded second base, the mind-numbing chant assaulting me from all sides, I found myself looking into the equally bewildered eyes of "Jack Nicholson", whom I had not spoken to since arriving the previous night.

He shook his head numbly, and as I headed for third base his one-word commentary once again echoed reassuringly in my ears:

"Bi-zarrrre!"

Even the dead hours of night were eventful at Boonville. All night long, bodies shifted mysteriously about the Chicken Palace, as vehicles spirited new people in and others away.

"Go to the barn!" someone would command in a whisper and more figures would shuffle away like ghouls to a graveyard. "The rest of you wait here."

By morning about a third of the faces I had bedded down with had changed. When the strains of "Red Red Robin" came filtering through my light veil of sleep, I decided to make this my last day at Boonville.

The previous evening's routine had ended much as it had begun with a barrage of singing, chanting and confession. Supper, like the previous meals, was a tasty combination of starches with hardly a grain of protein. Former camp cook Virginia Mabrey later told me the meals had been budgeted at 50 cents a day per person.

Dinner had been followed by self-generated entertainment, largely a collection of wholesome solo performances broken only by a raucous tune presented by Keith, a Loafers Glory favourite known as "A frog on a log in a bog in the fog". It was greeted by tepid applause from the otherwise vociferous project members.

The evening closed with a new activity: an intense group prayer directed to "Heavenly Father", which recruits were not asked to participate in, only "respect".

"Even if you don't believe in God, you can see the need for a central system of good values which are absolute, unchanging and eternal," Bethie had explained to us to reduce our surprise at the prayer.

"We use the word God to identify the source of those powers. So in reality, prayer is just a conversation you have with yourself."

Other religious terms had also come up during the lectures and been neutralized by their constant repetition. A "Messiah", for instance, was "someone who understands the historical forces at work at a certain point in history, and focuses them toward a single goal—for instance Gandhi or Buddha or Mao." The words "love" and "serve" had also become so interchangeable that I hardly noticed the difference any more. "A better world" seemed like a term I had used all my life.

Now, on the second day, I hardly had time to yawn before I was lugged from bed and back into the numbing routines of Moonie life. This second day, however, I was assigned a shadow, a pleasant enough fellow named Bruce who casually thudded along beside me wherever I went, even to the bathroom, talking nonstop.

Fortunately, by this time I had developed a number of small tricks to preserve my sanity—minute gestures that somehow helped me to maintain my sense of self. I found that I could avoid holding hands during singing if I grabbed one of the family song books and held it for my "brothers" and "sisters" to see, an unselfish gesture that kept one of my hands mercifully occupied for a precious half hour.

The unsettling stare of the Moonies could be beaten back by relentlessly returning it with seeming sincerity. Good eyes and reflexes helped me snatch salt, pepper and the like before five eager Moonies could do it for me. I even gained a bit of satisfaction during lectures by silently chanting silly little ditties like:

"You'll never get me, you'll see, you'll see.
You'll never get me, hee hee."

In retrospect this seems ridiculous, but it is astonishing to recall how important these tricks seemed then, when I felt every fibre of my person being sucked into this anonymous collectivity. The overload of information and emotion made the pull of the group so strong that at times, inexplicably, I felt like giving in myself, despite what I knew. Maybe the Moonies *were* right: maybe I was too cynical, too blase and negative. Maybe I *should* try letting myself "go with the flow" and see where it went. Wasn't I always the "neutral" journalist—playing it safe from the sidelines?

But no sooner did I entertain such feelings than I conjured up Benji's face at the restaurant—its blank, vacant features a beacon that warned me of the precipice at the end of the Moonie route. Something I had always taken for granted—the right to moments of private space inside my own head to sort things out—had proved far more important than I had ever imagined. Without those seconds of "spacing out", my thoughts seemed to buffet each other like waves in a storm, flooding my mental processes and short-circuiting my normal thinking.

Several bright and apparently "normal" people who came up with me were clearly swayed by the group's indoctrination techniques, shedding their critical faculties in the intense environment. Even stalwarts like "Nicholson" and Keith grew unusually silent and pensive during the urgency of the moving final lecture, late in the second full day.

Using time charts and various authorities as references, the lecturer traced historical periods of "darkness" and "light", weaving an analysis that made the present seem like the culmination of history. Mankind's history had peaked: technology could take man to the moon, education was nearly universal, transport connected even the remotest villages, communication systems linked the most foreign of people. Nuclear war hung like a sword on a thread over the entire dream. America was the Mecca of the world, San Francisco the Mecca of America—the starting point for the beats, the hippies, the anti-war movement, and now...

"Columbus knew he could cross the ocean...but what did they say?"

"Ah...you're nuts!" came the familiar refrain, and to my

surprise several recruits—including "Nicholson"—had joined in.

"And they were right: he *was* nuts. Like our ancestors, the pioneers were nuts to think they could cross the Rocky Mountains. Imagine...THE ROCKY MOUNTAINS...it's amazing! Why they must have been crazy.

"Well, there's a new kind of craziness around—it's called hope—and it's going to change the world."

"Ya-a-ayyyy!"

The energy in the room was so high I could feel it pulsing through me, and I found even myself wanting to believe in this crazy sheer idealism. It was all so ridiculous, but after nearly forty-eight hours in this twilight reality, our egos battered by confusion, our minds numbed by information—anything seemed possible.

"It's so simple," whispered a pleasant dark-haired girl beside me who had been a member for several weeks, "So easy." Others were hearing the lecture for their two-hundredth time, yet still found something "new" and "exciting" to garner from it.

Bethie asked everyone to join in a song and prayer, and I was amazed to find that the choice was "America, America," sung with the intensity of Birchers—eyes closed, mouths wide open, tears dripping down cheeks. During the prayer that followed, every recruit in the room but Keith had his eyes closed too, and beside me, my shadow Bruce was praying feverishly.

As he did, a fly landed on his lower lip, then slowly crawled inside his mouth, disappearing from view for a full dozen seconds. Bruce did not flinch.

It was in the immediate wake of this "high" that the Moonies pressured recruits to stay "just" one more day.

"You owe it to yourself to give it a try. What else have you got to do that's all that important? Are you too arrogant to even give it a try?" pressed older members in a spiel that mixed guilt with promise.

Keith was promised a job as a handyman on the farm; I a spot with a new newspaper they were starting up. I do not know what other recruits in my group were promised—but many ex-Moonies have testified that lying is routine at this point, as family members make use of personal information they have garnered during "sharing" sessions.

Disillusioned teachers are told they can work in the Project's alternative school (non-existent); single people see the promise of an interesting sexual relationship (unfulfilled); shy people find a flood of intimate new friends (temporary).

"If you're into rock music, they have a band; into health food, they have an organic farm," Tony Gillard had warned me as I left San Francisco, "and if you're into skateboarding down high mountains—they just happen to be doing that too. They'll say anything to make you stay, anything!"

Despite the pressure and my own curiosity, I did not stay longer. Earlier conversations with former members had given me some idea of what lay ahead. Those who agreed to stay "another" day would be shunted aboard a virtual boxcar, with the route ahead as unflinching as railroad tracks; given my confusion after only two days at Boonville, I did not want to risk any more.

I knew that after another exhausting day at Boonville, recruits would be convinced to attend a five day seminar at Camp K another isolated Moonie location where "3000 years of history" would be explained by an "incredible" lecturer, and where the hints and tidbits recruits had so far been receiving would crystallize into a "blinding understanding of life."

I knew that control techniques would be intensified too; further creating the environment of a giant Skinner box. Soon recruits would find themselves "jumping it" from bed instantly at morning wake-up; "clunking it" at night, when they would be expected to plunge into darkness moments after daily routine was over. Nothing would be forcing them to follow but peer pressure, the desire to avoid non-conformity when "ninety-nine people are doing one thing...

and you're doing another."

I knew recruits would soon be singing louder, chanting harder, even sacrificing food and sleep to keep up with the example of those about them. Self-hypnotic techniques would be taught to them, supposedly to increase their concentration, in reality to further blot out the capacity for critical thought.

"Stop it...stop it...STOP IT!" recruits would learn to repeat silently, whenever "negative" thoughts intruded —the final step in eradicating "spacing out", the first step in clearing the mind for a chain of apparent logic that would eventually alter their personalities completely.

I still did not know what that chain of logic was, or exactly how it affected people—but its intensity and effectiveness were held in awe by every former member I had spoken with. Somehow, reality would shift a few degrees. Isolation, dwindling sleep, little protein, constant confessions and no time to re-evaluate their circumstances would cause the recruits increasingly to lose perspective. They would never really decide to stay at the camp—they would defer indefinitely the decision to leave.

If they stayed long enough, the religious elements of the camp would sink in according to those with whom I had talked. Recruits would begin to feel special—in touch with some kind of "force"—and might even have religious dreams before dreaming stopped altogether in the later weeks. And when Rev. Moon's name began to come up in lectures two weeks later, six weeks later, or whenever they were deemed "ready" for it, it would no longer seem to matter as much as it would have earlier.

Day by day, Moon would become more important, his ideas more present, until one day it would seem only natural—a sudden revelation, coming perhaps in a dream—to realize he was the Messiah, responsible for their new lives.

They would become Moonies.

Yet for all the power of Boonville's indoctrination technique, I discovered that it could be interrupted in the early stages if the "program" was disturbed.

Late in my second full day at Boonville, I could see that several recruits, including "Jack Nicholson", were being persuaded to stay longer. I decided to interfere; during discussion of the last lecture of the day, I asked Bethie in public just whom it was the group followed.

Bethie hesitated at first, mentioning Jesus, Buddha and the psychiatrist Maslow "among others, of course"; but finally she reluctantly, if honestly, allowed that some of their teachings "originated" with Reverend Moon. Then she quickly launched into a lecture that would normally have come two weeks later in the program, explaining that Moon was an "interesting" man who had been "unfairly persecuted."

"All great men have been persecuted," she reminded us with a smile, "so much so that I sometimes think people aren't *really* worth listening to if they're not persecuted...ha ha."

Then, sensing the immediate negative response among new recruits, she backtracked, assuring us that the Project wasn't *really* connected with Moon anyway; they only studied some of his teachings. But it was too late—the name of Sun Myung Moon, notorious on the West Coast, was out of the bag too soon, and the results were irreversible.

Soon after this disclosure Nicholson told Bethie he wanted to leave Boonville. Bethie argued with him for more than half an hour, but he was determined to go even if it meant hitch-hiking back to San Francisco. As he passed me on the way out, he quietly drawled: "Thanks for that last question, pal..."

Accompanying him was a fellow who had been there for five days and was on the brink of signing up for a week-long session at Camp K. Now he refused steadfastly to stay any longer, maintaining that the connection with Moon made him feel he had some thinking to do. One after another in the hours that followed, other recruits left too, despite the pressuring, begging and cajoling of the Moonies. "Negativity" had found its way into Boonville, and nothing the Moonies could do would chase it away.

By the end of the day only Keith and I remained, and soon I was sprung by a pre-planned "emergency" call from Marilyn, notifying me that a close relative was ill. As I prepared to leave, Keith gave me a knowing wink and packed his rucksack to accompany me.

As the two of us marched toward the entry gate, all the Moonies lined up in neat rows to sing us a song, then Bethie hugged us warmly and begged us once more to remain and "give it a chance".

I looked into her piercing blue eyes and her incandescent smile, then back at the rest of the Moonies waving, singing and smiling at us. For one crazy moment I felt inexplicably touched and attracted to them again.

Then I turned quickly, followed by Keith, and trudged down the dusty road, past the gate and the sentry post. By the time I reached a nearby highway, only one thought stuck firmly in my exhausted mind: if Benji had been through five months at Boonville, there was no telling what it had done to his mind and his feelings for friends like me.

5

Two days later, Marilyn and I were back in Montreal, facing the hardest task that either of us could recall: telling Benji's parents of their son's predicament. During our two weeks in California, the Millers had phoned several of our friends seeking information about their long-absent son. No one had told them about our own involvement, in hope that Marilyn and I would return with Benji—but now we knew that the time had come. The day after our return, we invited the Millers to Lenny and Janet's home to fill them in.

Libby Miller, Benji's mother, was an open, talkative woman—by most standards, a somewhat typically suburban mother. Tall and attractive, with tinted blonde hair and a pale complexion, she worked part-time in a camping gear store and filled her spare time doing volunteer work in her community. But her principle interest was the well-being of her three children: Janice, a gangly teenager, preparing to enter college; Debbie, an aspiring pianist, practising music therapy in Europe; and Benji—the eldest and most independent, who she never stopped hoping would settle down with a wife and career.

Charles Miller was a warm, good humoured man, as predictable a father as Libby was a mother. An executive in the fashion industry, he boasted a small clothing line with the Miller name; but to friends and family, he was simply "Charlie"—a paunchy, balding man with an elfin smile, a fast wit and an unlimited supply of one-line jokes.

"How does the labor leader begin a bedroom story?" he asked us, seconds after entering Janet and Lenny's home. We hardly had time to catch our breath before the reply:
"Once upon a time-and-a-half."

The pair arrived exactly on time, he carefully attired in a suit and tie; she in a smart white dress; as we had predicted, they brought along a freshly-purchased coffee cake, which remained untouched throughout the evening's talk.

Gently but straightforwardly, we laid out our tale, from Mike's disappearance and return, through my own experience at Boonville. Though the details of our story were clearly a shock, their son's dilemma was not a complete surprise. Since Benji's departure, the Millers too had had their share of strange letters, dwindling in numbers, and abrupt phone calls with no details of the "Project".

"Everything was so secretive and mysterious," recalled Mrs. Miller. "Benji kept saying it was such a great place...but he couldn't tell us one word about it! We didn't know what it was he was involved in, but both of us had that feeling that it wasn't very good."

Overall, it was the grimmest evening I ever spent, watching the two parents exchange pained glances and struggle to hold back tears. When we finished our story, each of them had a rush of questions. Mrs. Miller's concerns were fairly motherly: how did Benji look? What was he wearing, how were his weight and complexion? Was there any possibility that he might be happy?

For Mr. Miller, it was nuts and bolts: what were the legal options? Who was behind the Moon organization? And most importantly—what were the chances of getting Benji out?

We answered their questions as candidly as possible—though I concealed one bit of information from them, and everyone else: I had little hope of seeing Benji again. My own stay in Boonville had badly demoralized me and left me in awe of the Moonie techniques. I had had several nightmares about Boonville since leaving the camp; now the whole trip seemed like a terrible nightmare, and I was chilled at the prospect of returning to San Francisco again.

Well after 2 a.m., we accompanied the Millers to the door of Lenny's flat, where they smiled graciously and thanked us for our help. They descended the stairs with remarkable poise, but watching them through the window, we could see them collapse in each other's arms, when they reached their car.

Over the following two days, we spoke with the Millers often, and gave them our files on Sun Myung Moon. They devoured our information and increased its scope with phone calls of their own—to San Francisco lawyers and police and to anti-Moon forces in a dozen states. Moved by their efforts, my own spirits began to rise, and I went back to the telephone to look into the committee headed by Rep. Donald Fraser that was already investigating Moon's political ties. Soon, with a few press contacts and a little luck, I came up with a Washington connection who promised me plenty of new information in the days to come.

But even before he returned my call, the Millers had learned more than they cared to know about Rev. Moon. Within three days of our return, they put forward their feelings, and everyone was in accord: we had to see Benji alone for long enough to talk to him. Since our own visit had been utterly in vain, and legal recourse was impossible, there was only one thing left for us to do. We would have to kidnap Benji.

"What else can we do?" asked a distraught Mrs. Miller. "Maybe we're acting like crazy parents...but I don't want to take the chance. If it's still our Benji, I think he'll understand."

We needed to lure Benji out, and fortunately, we had some bait: Benji's sister Debbie was visiting from Europe. A diligent, serious young woman of 26, Debbie was as different from her carefree brother as one could imagine, yet more surprised at his disappearance than anyone else. Benji was her "big brother"—a strong-willed, even-tempered, independent person whom she had always admired.

"I could imagine this happening to dozens of people I've met," she told us privately, "but not to him...not Benji! We've got to find a way to talk to him."

Several days after our initial encounter with her parents, Debbie Miller sat alone in the family basement and telephoned her brother at Washington House. According to the woman who answered, Benji was "away", but would call her back upon his return. The next day he did—his voice impassive, but his words indicating that he was pleased to hear his sister had returned.

According to plan, Debbie told him she would be visiting Vancouver to see an old friend, and she asked Benji to meet her there. He declined quickly, as it was "impossible" for him to leave California—but after a momentary pause, he invited Debbie to visit him. She asked for time to think it over, and Benji promised to call back the next day.

By the time his return call came, more than two days later, we had devised our plan. At first, Benji's invitation had seemed just the opening we needed, but on closer inspection it was a bigger risk than we could afford to take. While the old Benji would genuinely have wanted to see his sister, Benji the Moonie might have other motives: more than likely he would see Debbie as a potential Moonie, and whisk her up to Boonville at the very first chance.

No one was prepared to see Debbie go alone; the last thing the Millers needed was a second child to extricate from the cult. We had to find a way to get Debbie to California, without the possibility of a Boonville trip—and soon, a solution became clear.

When Benji's second call came, Debbie told him that Mrs. Miller was anxious to join her for the trip. But to keep the pot sweet, she assured him that their mother would stay for only three days, while Debbie would remain another week, alone. The possibility of luring Debbie up to Boonville once her mother had left, was obvious; after a brief silence, Benji jumped at the bait. When Debbie hung up several minutes later, Benji had agreed to pick up both sister and mother at San Francisco airport in four days time.

That night we gathered at the Miller's home to assemble a kidnap team, though it soon became apparent that our resources were lean. A reluctant volunteer, I was nonetheless everyone's first draft choice, as Marilyn could not go and no one else had been to San Francisco. Lenny, an old friend of Benji, agreed to accompany me, and Gary, a film teacher, and Simon, a union representative, hesistantly volunteered to round out our troupe.

As kidnappers went, we were a sorry collection: four balding pacifists, all pushing 30, with nary a fist fight between us since our public school days. Even if we did have the brains to plot a decent kidnapping, somebody else would have to provide the brawn. Our only hope was that we would find lots of help among our many friends in San Francisco.

Benji's father, Charlie, would also join us for the trip—as we would need his assistance once we got our hands on Benji. But that moment seemed far off indeed; with little more than a vague idea of what we would do once we arrived, our strange crew made its reservations to fly to San Francisco and kidnap Benji.

As we left the Miller's home that final evening and went our separate ways, all of us were nervous and unsure about the coming days' venture. But by the following morning we were even more perturbed, for during the night I had received a phone call from my Washington connection, who told me everything that he had learned about the forces behind Moon.

When our plane flew off into the western sky the next afternoon, we knew a great deal more about our Korean adversary. His influence was far greater and closer to home than any of us had imagined.

6

On a June day in 1965, a limousine pulled into the spacious Gettysburg farm of Dwight D. Eisenhower, retired president of the United States.

Out of the car stepped a delegation sent by Ike's old friend Yang You Chan, former South Korean ambassador to the U.S.: the group included several young Korean dancers known as the "Little Angels", accompanied by a rotund man introduced as a Korean minister.

"You are well armed with cameras, I see," joshed the elderly ex-president, as shutters clicked. "And what is the name of your movement?"

"The Unification Church," clucked the Korean evangelist, as his handsome assistant Bo Hi Pak pulled out a glossy biography of Moon, including photos of a recent 124-couple wedding he had conducted. Eisenhower's eyes grew "round", according to a Unification Church magazine describing the incident.

"Never saw anything quite like this before," said the surprised ex-president, who spent the next 45 minutes amiably chatting with his guests before the limousine disappeared down the road again. For Ike, the meeting was just another interruption in a pleasant Pennsylvania day; but for the man in the car—Sun Myung Moon—it was a crucial encounter; the first tiny wedge in a crack that would eventually open a broad passageway to some of the most powerful people in the United States.

Soon after the meeting, Eisenhower agreed to become the "honorary president" of the Korean Cultural Freedom Foundation (KCFF), supposedly an organization to fight communism and promote Korean-American cultural ties: in reality, a front group for the Unification Church.

Using this key endorsement from Ike, Bo Hi Pak soon milked similar endorsements from former president Harry Truman, dozens of senators and congressmen including Richard Nixon and Gerald Ford, and eventually a Who's Who of American personalities such as Bob Hope, Bing Crosby and Ed Sullivan.

These sponsors in turn opened the taps to some million dollars a year in KCFF contributions from 140,000 Americans trying to fight the "Red menace"—a flow of money that would remain undammed until 1975, when the group's links to Moon finally became known.

But by that time, the cloak over the KCFF was expendable; Rev. Sun Myung Moon had many more irons in the fire...

Slightly more than a year after our kidnap team left Montreal, the U.S. Congressional Committee headed by then Rep. Donald Fraser would conclude its lengthy investigation of Moon's political empire. Fraser would find that Moon had been one of the key components in a vast attempt by the South Korean Government to influence U.S. domestic and foreign policy, and that Moon in turn had used both the Korean Government and an astonishing number of prominent American personalities to further his own goal—which was no less than to "get hold of the whole world".

The committee's findings would seem an extraordinary list of accomplishments for a fringe cult whose leader had long been the object of ridicule. But they would come as no surprise to us—only confirming publicly what we had learned a year earlier from our friends in San Francisco and from our Washington connection: that parallelling Moon's complex financial organization, is an even more complex and murky political empire, the full extent of which may never be known. Some of the components of that political empire uncovered by

Journey Into the Mind of a Cult 81

the Fraser Committee are outlined in the following pages.

Korean Cultural Freedom Foundation (KCFF)

Once Eisenhower and Truman were persuaded to become honorary presidents, fourteen generals, eight admirals and an army of American personalities clambered onto the KCFF's "advisory board".

Their endorsements enabled the KCFF to churn out PR material befitting Bicentennial Day, asking for money to "fight communism" and help save "starving Korean children". Thousands of prominent Americans were taken in, among them George Meany, Jack Nicklaus, Johnny Unitas and Rep. Carl Albert. The owners of Reader's Digest alone gave the KCFF half a million dollars.

The only critical voice came from the U.S. embassy in Korea, which continually warned that the KCFF was a front group for "unsavory people"—but the U.S. Government took no action.

In 1976 a New York State agency audited one of the KCFF's charitable ventures, The Childrens' Relief Fund, and found that only two per cent of the $1.2 million collected that year had gone to hungry children. They banned the KCFF from soliciting in New York, and slowly the national spotlight focused on the organization.

By 1978, the KCFF's blood links with Moon and the Unification Church were completely known and its profits and power greatly reduced. However, Bo Hi Pak still operates the KCFF and continues to claim it has "no connection to Moon".

The KCFF also gave birth to other projects, notably the "Little Angels"—a colorful Korean childrens' dance troupe that did wonders for Moon's prestige. Moon conceived the group in 1962, then turned it over to the KCFF which soon had support from the Korean Government.

Moon hoped the group would someday spread his influence into the "palaces of kings and queens", and it almost did. The Little Angels had a private audience with Queen Elizabeth in Buckingham Palace, and were the first cultural group to appear before the United Nations. They played with stars like Sammy Davis Jr. and Liberace, in concert halls from Carnegie Hall to Africa, and recorded an album with MGM.

The concerts provided Moon the opportunity to mingle and have his picture taken with politicians and diplomats. These photos were added to his growing stock of PR material to further enhance his image as a world-respected figure with powerful friends.

The third major KCFF project, a brainchild of Bo Hi Pak, was Radio Free Asia (ROFA)—a radio outlet intended to broadcast to the "suffering millions" behind the bamboo curtain. This venture also attracted millions of dollars of private American money, until 1975, when its close links with the Korean Government and Moon became public. ROFA was discontinued soon afterwards.

Freedom Leadership Foundation (FLF)

The FLF is the Church's chief political arm in the U.S. It is registered as a non-profit educational organization, intended to "develop leadership" in the "struggle against communism".

When it was founded in the late sixties, it stirred protest among some early Church members who came from left-wing backgrounds. They were told that it was a religious command to begin political work in the United States.

"Thereafter, members' objections to political activity was considered infidelity to Master and was like being disobedient to God," says Alan Tate Wood, President of the FLF in 1970, and one of the topmost defectors from Moon's Church.

"North Korea's Strategy to Make New War...belligerent, warmongering tactics..." blared slick propaganda leaflets handed out by the FLF. "The U.S. must not fail...to defend

South Korea against communist aggression."

This anti-communist stand not only ingratiated Moon with the South Korean government but broadened his contacts with prominent Americans. FLF publications at the time contained photos of Moon meeting Ike, Humphrey, Thurmond, Kennedy, Nixon and other distinguished Americans.

FLF chapters were also set up in 40 countries, under an international Moon anti-communist front known as "Victory Against Communism" (VOC). In Japan Moonies compaigned for right-wing candidates during elections, in Vietnam they provided medical units, and in South Korea they set up the World Freedom Institute, a still-functioning anti-communist indoctrination centre to which Korean civil servants and army officers are sent annually for an overview of Communism.

But FLF President Neil Salonen, a top Moon spokesman, maintains that their anti-communist work and support of South Korea is not a function of political beliefs but rather of "spiritual, religious feelings".

"We don't lobby," says Salonen. "We educate."

One of the FLF's chief educational tools was the Washington lobby team—some twenty attractive, well groomed Moonie women who distributed tea, flowers and friendship at Capitol Hill until 1977.

Operating out of an old manor several blocks from the Capitol, the teams lobbied congressional staff on issues of concern to Moon, and tried to form personal relationships with staff members on any pretext they could.

"They were sweet girls, they put you at ease. They sent you flowers," New York State Senator Israel Ruiz said of his encounter with them during Moon's 1976 God Bless America festival. "They were the most terrific propagandists I've ever encountered."

Moon's speeches to his members hardly concealed the purpose of the lobby: "Master needs many good-looking girls—three hundred. He will assign three girls to each senator...if our girls are superior to the senator in many ways, then the senators will just be taken by our members.

"If we find among the senators and congressmen no one really usable for our purpose, we can make senators and congressmen of our members. This is our dream—our project—but shut your mouth tight and have hope and go on to realize it. We must have an automatic theocracy to rule the world."

The team rented a special suite at the Washington Hilton at which they entertained receptive congressmen and staff. The girls were well-trained, and encouraged to use deceptive tactics, justifying them by the Moonie motto: "Be as wise as serpents and as innocent as doves."

"The implication was to be persistent and cunning—anything to make him like you so he'd become a friend and ally," recalls one former member of the lobby team. "It was very effective."

The Fraser Committee concluded that it was hard to say how successful the team was in getting to members of Congress, but some of their achievements are worth noting. At least two members of the team, Sherry Westerledge and Susan Bergman, were employed on the staff of congressmen until 1979, though they continued to live at the Church headquarters and turn over their salary.

Miss Bergman, who worked for Rep. Doug Hammerschmidt, won attention in 1976 for her curious relationship with the former Speaker of the House, Carl Albert. The pretty, hazel-eyed Miss Bergman would bring Albert flowers each morning, then brew him ginseng tea in his office and later accompany him around Capitol Hill. Albert came under criticism for his actions but he insisted that Miss Bergman was "just a nice girl, a very nice girl, a Jewish girl from New York. She got all hepped up on Jesus and she just wants to share it. I think that's a nice thing. I think she wants to convert me."

As a result of the lobby team's efforts, Moon himself was able to penetrate Capitol Hill on several occasions, notably for a prayer meeting in his honor held in the House Caucus

Room by Congressmen Bill Chappell and Richard Ichord. Moon arrived for the affair in a resplendent black Lincoln and was trailed by bodyguards down the congressional halls to the Caucus Room. According to Time Magazine, Rep. Ichord then said he was "profoundly impressed" with the church group and "broadly compared the millionaire clergyman to Moses, John the Baptist and Jesus".

The lobby team has not been active in Washington since the end of 1977, but many of its members now belong to PR teams that travel the country explaining the Church and its principles to local politicians, university students and businessmen.

Operation Watergate

The best known of the Church's political activities was its effort to save Nixon during Watergate, a campaign which eventually gained Moon entry to the Oval Office.

Dubbed "Project Archangel Nixon", the lobby began in November 1973 with full-page newspaper ads in 21 cities calling on readers to "Forgive, Love, Unite...God has chosen Richard Nixon...We must love the President of the United States". These ads were followed by a forty-day Prayer and Fast Vigil on the steps of the Capitol Hill and intense lobbying by the Washington team, which secured the signatures of 28 congressmen and 4 senators to endorse their fast. One congressman read an "inspirational appeal" by Moon into the record.

Subsequently, Moon's Watergate Committee was called by President Nixon's secretary and invited to attend the annual White House Christmas Tree Lighting Ceremony December 14th. Twelve hundred Moonies showed up, demonstrating for the beleaguered president in a well-rehearsed display.

Transcripts of Church documents obtained by the Fraser Committee record Church leaders drilling members on how to behave. "Small, intimate personal things can make a large impact...On camera, medium prayer looks very good. Very strong prayer doesn't. It looks strange...don't clench your fists when you are singing."

That night the Moonies returned for a candlelight vigil during which Tricia Nixon and husband Edward mingled with the crowd and offered their thanks. Similar demonstrations were held by Moonies in Japan, Germany, Italy, England and other U.S. cities.

Soon after, Moon was invited by the president's office to the annual Prayer Breakfast for religious leaders on February 1, 1974. Later that day he met privately with Nixon for thirty minutes in the Oval Office, where he reportedly hugged the President and prayed fervently over him in Korean. A few months later, Moon told his followers:

"If this dying person, Nixon, is revived, then Reverend Moon's name will be more popular and famous, right?"

An interesting footnote to the Watergate Project is the possibility that lobbyists were also gathering information on individual congressmen. Each Moonie lobbyist was assigned 23 congressmen and told to keep an index card on each, citing "every time the congressman saw you, spoke to you...including the time, location and circumstance. Describe your interaction in detail."

Why was the information gathered?

"It was all in the interest of the Mission—with a capital M," a former member of the lobby team told me. "But I had no idea what that Mission was...I just followed the orders of the higher-ups."

International Conference for the Unity of the Sciences (ICUS)

Moon's major thrust at the scientific community, ICUS is an annual event that gathers hundreds of academics from around the world to discuss "The Search for Absolute Values".

The conference is a ritzy affair: all travel, food and lodging costs are picked up by Moon, and the bill usually reaches $500,000. Some guests refuse to come when they learn th~

conference is sponsored by Moon, but many others aren't bothered in the least.

In 1978, the affair was held in the days following the People's Temple suicide in Guyana; nonetheless, ninety per cent of those invited showed up, including four Nobel Prize laureates and other notables like Paolo Soleri, Karl Pribham and Kasim Gulek, former prime minister of Turkey.

Outside the hotel, protesters carried placards asking "Scientists! Where are your ethics? Where are your values?"

Inside, debate focused on everything from "Health Problems in West Africa" to "Etiologic and Immunologic Aspects in Nasopharyngeal Cancer". The most striking workshop was one entitled "Death and Suicide in Contemporary Thought"—a 2-1/2 hour session during which, astonishingly, the days-old tragedy in Guyana was never mentioned, despite newspapers littering the conference floor announcing that the death toll had climbed to 775. Instead, scientists mulled over debate on "romantic suicides" by Sylvia Plath and Plato's Socrates: the main paper, by author Joyce Carole Oates, was on "The Art of Suicide".

Most participants, like Nobel physics laureate Eugene Wigner, termed it "irrelevant" that the conference was sponsored by Moon. Others were more lavish in their remarks: MIT sociologist Daniel Lerner praised the Moonies as "among the greatest young people we have today".

Several hundred Moonies were brought to the conference, in buses labelled "Aboji Monsei" (Victory for Father). Looking like they shared the same tailor and barber, the well-groomed youngsters sat watching the affair with a curious but impressed expression while higher-ups mingled with the scientists. After all, that's what the conference was for. As Master Speaks explains:

"If we invite them (the scientists) on the pretext of giving these lectures they will be touched by the students, then they will want the students in their university to go through this type of training. Before long, without money we will influence the whole of the United States by influencing the intellectuals first...We will surely influence the policies of the whole world, in the near future."

The Fraser Committee characterized ICUS as part of Moon's overall strategy of controlling major institutions around the world. Moon also speaks of setting up a Unified Economists Conference, a World Politicians Conference and a World Media Conference.

He has also promised to establish a "prize system" more prestigious than the Nobel Prize, and has pledged to build his own university. Land in New York has already been purchased for it.

Korean, KCIA Connection

Who, if anyone, is behind Rev. Moon? Does he actually believe he is the Messiah, or does he represent larger interests?

Many ex-Moonies I have spoken with are convinced that Moon does indeed believe in his own power as Messiah. Their opinion seems to be supported by Moon's own personal behavior and by the sheer flamboyance of many of his speeches.

Even Bo Hi Pak, Moon's right-hand man and liaison with the South Korean Government, seems to be a "true believer": according to Judy Stanley, Pak registered his own son in Barrytown's 100-day "training program" on the day he turned sixteen. Many other leaders particularly those in the lower echelons, seem to be thoroughly indoctrinated.

Yet despite their convictions, there is far more to Moon and Pak than religion. The Fraser Committee found them to be at the centre of South Korean government schemes to influence the United States.

Don Ranard, former director of the State department's office of Korean Affairs told me: "Moon and Pak may both be on the strange side, but even if they are...they know exactly what they're doing. They have friends and influence in all kinds of high places and they represent a lot more than the Unification Church."

To understand Moon's political roots, one has to know something of South Korea since 1961, when Park Chung Hee overthrew the constitutional government of that country and installed a military dictatorship.

Propping up the Park regime was the omnipresent KCIA, described by one U.S. State department man as "a state within a state, a shadowy world of...bureaucrats, intellectuals, agents and thugs".

Established in 1961 with the aid of the American CIA, the KCIA has since earned a reputation as one of the most brutal and repressive security forces in the world. With an estimated force of 50,000 men and women, the KCIA controls all aspects of life in South Korea: nothing is printed or broadcast without their approval; politicians, labor leaders, government officials, clergymen and students are all watched, and sometimes arrested, beaten and killed.

These are the swampy waters from which Moon has emerged intact, well-groomed and very influential; his relationship with South Korean authorities unclear, but evidently good. Consequently, many critics have accused Moon of being a direct agent of the KCIA, a charge which Bo Hi Pak brands as "Trash, total lies, distorted and vicious in nature."

In its report, the Fraser Committee stopped short of saying that Moon was an agent for the South Korean Government, but it concluded that there was at least a "collaborative relationship" between the two parties. Moon was given freedom of movement and often support for his ventures by the South Korean government; in return he worked consistently in its interests, and sometimes under its direct orders.

In the words of former FLF president Alan Tate Wood, the goals of the Unification Church and the KCIA in the United States "overlap so thoroughly as to display no difference at all".

Moon's relationship with the KCIA began in 1962, when the agency's first chief, Kim Chong Pil, met secretly with a small group of North American Moonies at a San Francisco hotel. Two of Pil's top aides were already members of the Unification Church, and, over soft drinks, Pil is reported to have told the American group he would work behind the scenes for the Unification Church in both South Korea and America.

Three years later, while still directing the KCIA, Pil became honorary chairman of the Korean Cultural Freedom Foundation (KCFF), the Church's first front group in the United States.

According to the Fraser Committee, this cozy relationship between Moon and the Korean authorities continued in the years ahead. The South Korean government sponsored such Moon enterprises as Radio Free Asia and the Little Angels, and gave Bo Hi Pak access to the diplomatic pouch and cable in South Korea's U.S. Embassy. On one occasion the KCIA hired three Washington secretaries on the direct recommendation of Moon's FLF.

Moon has also been allowed to hold rallies in South Korea, and on at least one occasion was feted by South Korea's speaker of the House, who threw a banquet in Moon's honor.

In exchange, Moon's Washington lobby team worked to convince U.S. representatives to maintain the 40,000 troops and billions of dollars in aid that the U.S. sends to South Korea. They also staged rallies in support of Park in Korea and in the U.S., one of which the Fraser Report states was specifically ordered by the KCIA.

Moon's support of South Korea goes further. It is woven right into his Divine Principle, in which he teaches members that Korea is the Holy Motherland, the "second Israel", and Korean the holy language that everyone in the world will speak some day.

Moonies are encouraged to fight on the "front lines" of the Korean struggle and some members have even pledged to die in battle, disturbing parents who worry that Korea may use American Moonies.

As always, Moon's own words are hardly reassuring: in 1975 he told a huge rally in South Korea that in the event of another Korean war, Unification Church members "believe it is God's will to protect their Fatherland to the last, to organize the *Unification Crusade Army*, and take part in the war as a support force to defend both Korea and the free world". (My italics.)

Yet Moon's final vision seems to stretch much further than tiny Korea, which he views as little more than a launching pad for his overall strategy to "conquer and subjugate the world". In Master Speaks, Moon repeatedly states that he will take control of the world's institutions and create a "world theocracy" with himself as leader. He even warns of a final, cataclysmic battle in which:

"We should defeat Kim Il Sung (president of North Korea), smash Mao Tse Tung and crush the Soviet Union, in the name of God."

In the final analysis, Moon may work for South Korea in the short term, and may even be a direct agent of the South Korean government and the KCIA, but his dreams are far grander:

"My life is not so small that I would act as a KCIA agent. My eyes and goal are not just for Korea. America is the goal; the world is my goal and target."

Japan

One facet of Moon's political empire was not even touched upon by the Fraser Committee—the Japanese connection which some Moon-watchers believe to be more important than even the link with Korea. Moon's Japanese Church, the Genri Undo, is an influential movement tied to some of the most powerful ultra-right nationalist forces in Asia.

Moon's three principal backers in the Orient are Ryoichi Sasagawa, Nobusuke Kishi and Yoshio Kodama—post war billionaires and political forces who share a dream of restoring the Emperor and Japan to their former glory. Some observers believe they are the real power behind Moon.

Sasagawa is the godfather of the Japanese underworld and the founder of the Japanese kamikaze pilot squads. He was imprisoned briefly as a Class A war criminal after the war, then released to become a billionaire political power in Indonesia and Cambodia. He actively supports the Unification Church in Japan, and is described by Bo Hi Pak as a "true humanitarian and patriot", by Moon as "very close to Master".

Sasagawa was also at the centre of the old China Lobby—a powerful combination of Asian dictators, American right-wing politicians and international businessmen who influenced U.S. policy in the Pacific after World War II. In the 1960's Sasagawa set up the World Anti-Communist League (WACL), currently the major alliance of right-wing forces in the world. Moon's Japanese Church is a member of the WACL, and sponsored its 1970 annual conference. Moon claims his Church raised $1.4 million in flower sales and helped finance the "best WACL conference ever".

The man in charge of promoting that conference was Nobusuke Kishi another active backer of the Japan Unification Church, a former prime minister of Japan, and president of its ruling party. At the 1970 WACL meeting, Kishi organized a grand welcoming banquet for Moon when he arrived in Japan.

According to Bo Hi Pak, both Kishi and Sasagawa help the Unification Church by "encouraging young people through their position as elder statesmen. They open doors, issue statements and attend rallies, and they testify to other important Japanese."

The third member of this right-wing triumvirate, Yoshio Kodama, has been described by the New York Times as "one of the most powerful men in the Orient". He recently became notorious for his role in the Lockheed pay-off scandal involving the Japanese government.

Kodama is considered one of the kingpins of Japanese politics, and has had a hand in selecting several prime ministers. He is not an active Moon backer, but acted as an advisor to Kishi and the Moonies during the 1970 WACL meeting. Moon's links with Kodama, Kishi and Sasagawa have raised speculation that Japan is the source of his early funding; Harpers magazine even speculated that his seed money may have come through the Lockheed pay-offs, raising the possibility that Moon began his growth with American corporate funds.

Moon has at least two other interesting links in Japan. One is with recently defeated prime minister Takeo Fukuda, who attended a banquet in Moon's honour in 1974, accompanied by two cabinet ministers. When questioned in the Japanese Diet, Fukuda replied: "He (Moon) is a very splendid man, and his philosophy has common parts with my own—namely cooperation and unity. So I was very impressed by him."

Moon is also close to Japan's director of the environment, Shintaro Ishihara, who received enormous door-to-door support from the Moonies in the 1976 elections. Shortly after, Ishihara attended a Church dinner and announced: "I received great help from your people...in my election campaign. I had no idea there were such fine young people in present day Japan."

These links with some of the most powerful people in the Orient make many Moon watchers believe that Moon is more than a puppet for the Korean Government. According to Andrew Ross, a West Coast journalist who broke many of Moon's Korean connections long before the Fraser Committee. "Moon is right at the centre of a constellation of world-wide right-wing forces that is very powerful...and very frightening."

How powerful is the Church today?

Since the outset of the Fraser Committee, the South Korean Government has gone to great lengths to disassociate itself from Moon and the Church. It has cancelled the passports of the Little Angels ballet troupe and has charged the president of Moon's ginseng tea company with $6 million in tax evasion. (He escaped to Japan.)

The Church cites these difficulties as proof that it has no links with South Korea, while other critics have said it certainly spells the end of any "special relationship" Moon has enjoyed with the South Korean Government.

The Fraser committee found evidence, however, that as late as 1978 the Church continued to have "significant support" from South Korean authorities. The committee pointed out that in that year a Moon industry was awarded contracts as a chief weapons supplier for the Korean Government. They put particular emphasis on a strange incident that occured in late 1977: the American weapons firm Colt Industries sent a cable to the South Korean government suggesting an arms deal. Several weeks later Colt officials received a call from Moon's Tong-Il manufacturing plant. Moon's representatives then told Colt officials they would work out the deal for South Korea. They said the Korean government was aware of their actions and supported them, but would deny it if it came out in public.

The subcommittee recalled Moon's professed goals, including the formation of a "Unification Crusade Army", and concluded its report on this note:

"Under the circumstances, the subcommittee believes it is in the interests of the United States to know what control Moon and his followers have over instruments of war and to what extent they are in a position to influence Korean defence policies."

The assassination of South Korean president Park in late 1979 throws Moon's future status in Korea into question. No one can say whether the new government of Choi Kyu Hah will continue to favor Moon or simply consider him a nuisance. However, it is worth noting that one of the most powerful men in the new government, so powerful that he was considered a leading candidate to become president, is Kim Chong Pil; the man who met secretly with the Unification Church in San Francisco in 1961 and later became the honorary chairman of the KCFF.

In America too there are strong indications that Moon is far from dead. His financial investments continue to grow rapidly in fishing, film, newspaper and real estate, and his annual science conference continues to attract distinguished academics the world over. In November 1979, the ICUS science conference was held in Los Angeles and drew a full house.

Moon is again living in the United States after several months out of the country during the term of a subpoena by the Fraser Committee, and he is planning a mass wedding of two thousand couples in the United States sometime in 1980. He was also hoping to plan a giant "March on Moscow" in 1980—a top secret mission in which troops of Moonies would sweep down on the Russian Olympics in the guise of marching bands, with Divine Principles and bibles concealed in their drums.

Perhaps the most telling example of the Moonies' still-flourishing power was displayed against the man who has been most effective in exposing them—Rep. Donald Fraser.

In the 1978 primaries, the Moonies campaigned actively against Fraser in his home state of Minnesota. As the Fraser Committee noted, all aspects of the Moon organization were synchronized against him—political, economic and religious. Anti-Fraser brochures were printed up by Moon's publishing company; documentaries were made of the Fraser hearings by Moon film crews for airing in Korea; articles derogating Fraser and making Bo Hi Pak a martyr were run in News World; and individual Church members campaigned against Fraser in the street.

The results were effective. On October 7, about a month before the release of his committee's final report, Donald Fraser was narrowly defeated in his bid to become the Democratic candidate for the Senate.

Sun Myung Moon had proved a more powerful opponent than even Fraser could deal with.

7

It took us two days in San Francisco to round up our kidnap team. They were hardly the Magnificent Seven.

Four middle-aged doctors, a Carolina mountain man, a bald textile executive and an Italian private eye made unlikely kidnappers; but time was short and we couldn't be choosy.

Help had been gathered from rather eclectic sources. Keith, the drinking, thinking mountain man from Loafer's Glory was still in town and quickly volunteered to help. So did an old friend, Dr. M., an aging Montreal hippie practitioner who had fled Canada for what he termed the "three W's" of California—warmth, women and weed.

Other San Francisco friends we had counted on dropped out of our plans: one complaining of a nervous stomach, the other a "mild case of terror". Reluctantly, we agreed to let Benji's father participate in kidnapping his son from Father Moon.

Next I called Dr. David Leof, a portly Jungian psychiatrist I had consulted when I first returned from Boonville. My tale of the camp's psychology had so horrified him that he had promised he would "do anything" to help us out. He was as good as his word; the graying psychiatrist suspended an afternoon's appointments and a lifetime of pacifism to join our crew; as well, he enlisted the help of two polished friends, Dr. G. and Dr. F, prominent San Franciso physicians who normally specialized in kidneys, not kidnaps.

We still needed a seventh man: a private eye to give us advice and tip us off when Benji set foot in the airport. Then Benji's mother could lure him back to her hotel room, where the rest of us would be waiting to make the snatch.

"This is Mick Mazzoni's electronic answering service. Speak as long as you want, but keep it short," snapped the tape-recorded voice of the private eye we hoped to hire.

We had already tried a half dozen other detectives and come to some strange dead ends. One fellow was a brass knuckles type with a voice like a foghorn and an IQ to match; a second spoke to me from the rifle range, his words drowned out by the crack of gunfire. Still another was a pipe-smoking would-be Holmes, who filled our ears with analyses of the "criminal sect type".

Mazzoni was the first who fitted the bill. He'd been described to us as a "master of a thousand disguises"; as we waited to meet him outside our hotel lobby we scrutinized every passing old lady, convinced it was the chameleon-like detective.

When he finally arrived, and came to our room, his fairly ordinary appearance was a trifle disappointing, though his manner more than compensated. An ex-cop with the demeanor of a drill sergeant, Mazzoni had rugged, almost surly features, and a squared-off beard that I think was real. His army fatigues looked as though they'd been slept in, while his beady eyes constantly scanned the hotel room as though searching for a cache of plastic explosives.

"A good kidnapping is like fixing a flat tire," Mazzoni explained to us moments after hearing our plan. "There's no point doing it if you don't do it right."

Mazzoni gave us a number of tips, among them to replace our original getaway car with a two-door Cordoba. "The Cordoba", he said professorially, "has lots of room to stuff a body into the back seat, and the seat belts don't get in the way.

"It's a very good car for kidnapping."

Mazzoni also suggested we plant a "switch car" a couple of miles away, near Candlestick Park, in case our getaway car was spotted. He even told us how to align the cars during the switch (back to front) so that Benji could be transferred with minimum resistance.

Before leaving, Mazzoni insisted on teaching us a bit of judo—transforming our hotel room into a makeshift gym, bodies hurtling through the air and crashing into walls until our neighbors pounded on our door to complain.

"Pssst...take this," Mazzoni had whispered to me as he left, shoving a thin black tube of tear gas into my reluctant hands.

"If things get rough and you've got to get out, throw this and abort the mission."

Despite Mazzoni's advice, arranging the caper proved never-ending in its complications as we sallied about the city renting cars, soliciting help and racing back to our hotel to collect our messages. Strange as it was for Lenny, Gary, Simon and me, it was more so for Benji's father, usually found asleep in the back of the car.

Charlie, as we had come to know him, was a wreck; yet an admirable one, doing his best to cope with the painful situation. When he first paid Mazzoni, he broke into tears, overwhelmed by the macabre nature of the services he was buying. But in the days that followed he adapted remarkably well, keeping up with the frenetic pace, offering invaluable advice and even lounging about the hotel floor with us to eat pizza and drink scotch late into the night.

During the day Charlie burned off his nervous energy telling jokes to anyone who would listen.

"What do you call a honeymoon salad," he would ask our bewildered hotel waitress. "Come on...ask me what a honeymoon salad is."

(Silence.)

"Lett-uce alone."

An hour later he was slumped exhausted in the back seat of

the car again, his ever-present tie fluttering in the breeze, as we headed toward our next calamity.

Typical was our renting of the "switch" car. Watching the new car wheel out of the rental docks, Simon bit his lip and whispered to Lenny:

"Geez, what are we gonna do? It's another blue Cordoba!"

Lenny paled at the thought of jumping from one blue Cordoba to another.

"You're not going to believe this," he stammered to the girl at the counter, "but I *can't stand* blue. In fact I'm allergic to it!"

"Me too," added Simon, as the woman's eyes darted from one to the other.

"But what's the difference?" she asked, puzzled. "You've only rented it for *one day*."

"Yeah, I know," persisted Lenny. "It's just that I don't *like* blue."

Down at the far end of the counter, some businessmen were struck by this last remark.

"Ohhh," they lamented in unison. "That's too bad. He doesn't like blooooooo."

Several minutes later, the sales girl had convinced her disbelieving boss to send down "any colour but blue", and a shiny green Cordoba came rolling out.

"Green!" shouted Lenny and Simon ecstatically. "We just love green!"

Finding a suitable hotel to stage the snatch proved a major headache, since none of us knew the city. We wanted somewhere out of the way, with one exit that could be easily cut off by a couple of cars and some amateur kidnappers. The search took us from the poshest hotels to sleazy dives where schemes like ours were probably routine.

In one motel we slipped a pass key off the wall of the desk clerk and furtively roamed from room to room seeking the "perfect kidnap site", only to walk in on a couple in *flagrante delicto*. In another we were about to rent a second-floor room when Mr. Miller became terrified Benji might leap out the window. We quickly changed our plans.

Mazzoni had suggested we buy a heavy chain and padlock so we could fasten the Moonie vehicle's steering wheel to a pole after the kidnapping—a gentler method than slashing its tires or smashing the windshield. The mammoth chain trailed suspiciously behind us as we wandered through each hotel seeking a convenient pole.

After sixteen hours and dozens of hotels, we settled on a cozy if chintzy little place just off the freeway. We rented a room, then settled down to see what the traffic situation would be like when Mrs. Miller's airplane arrived at 5:30 the next day.

At 5 p.m. blondes in sports cars began pulling in and grinding their way up to the rooms. Minutes later men in large cars began to arrive and follow them up the stairs, while police cars completed the strange procession, drifting in and out of the parking lot like a stake-out.

"Good God," whispered a startled Charlie Miller. "It's a hooker's hotel!"

As we turned to flee, we discovered worse: the whole hotel was equipped with hidden cameras, recording our every move since we'd first arrived. We grabbed our padlock and left quickly, remembering to inquire at every further hotel to make sure there were no security arrangements.

Two hours later with night falling and a worn-out Mr. Miller long since asleep, we rented rooms at the Airport Holiday Inn. It was a bit high-profile for our purpose, and it had two entrances; but it was the best we could do in time for the plan. We took two adjacent rooms with a connecting door, one for Mrs. Miller to check into with Benji, the other for us to hide in.

Four weeks after the strange odyssey had begun, the trap was finally set.

Keith, whom we had counted on for muscle, never made it.

Hopping into a cab at his construction site an hour before the kidnapping was scheduled, he offered the cabbie a $10 tip and was most of the way to the hotel when the car blew a tire and skidded off the road. He ended up jogging along the highway in his construction boots and hard hat, passing stalled traffic and covering several miles, but it was too late. By the time he arrived everyone was gone except the police, who were at the hotel to investigate a kidnapping.

It was a bungled job right from the start. Fifteen minutes before the kidnapping was planned, *no one* had shown up except us and Dr. M., causing much consternation. At the last minute Dr. Leof wheeled in with his Mercedes, his wife and his five-year-old son in tow. He also brought Dr. G. and Dr. F., swaddled in expensive three-piece suits as though they were off to a medical convention.

We hastily outlined our plan to them, then took up our posts. We had four cars at our disposal and we used them to occupy most of the nearby hotel parking spaces, forcing Benji and whatever Moonies accompanied him to park directly in front of our room.

Dr. Leof and his family parked outside the room as well, unloading baggage like busy vacationers. Nearby, Dr. G. sat casually in another vehicle, waiting to cut the Moonies off in front, while Benji's father manned a third car, ready to spirit away his wife and daughter.

Even Dr. Leof's tiny son was armed with a tire valve. "Take zis, Anton," his chic Parisienne mother had told him. "If the bad man tries to get away—phffft—you let ze air out of his tire!"

On the far side of the lot, Dr. M. was waiting nervously in the getaway car. As he sat there drumming his fingers against the dashboard, a Holiday Inn van parked directly in front of him, blocking the escape route. Dr. Leof came coolly to the rescue.

"I'm a psychiatrist here to seize a dangerous patient," he bluffed the van's driver, flashing a card. "The FBI is here with me—please move."

Meanwhile Mr. Miller, Dr. F. and the four of us crouched in the darkened hotel room, peering through a crack in the curtain at some chubby women practising putts on a hotel golf green. It was 5:45 and the plane had landed fifteen minutes earlier, yet we still hadn't heard from Mazzoni at the airport. The waiting was becoming unbearable.

The phone rang. It was Mazzoni.

"Benji's here with another Moonie," he said tersely. "They've picked up Mrs. Miller in a 1976 Mustang. Get ready!"

Several minutes later we were all nervous wrecks, when Simon broke the silence with a hoarse whisper.

"I see it...a silver Mustang. It's coming right this way."

A car stopped directly in front of the window.

I strained to peek through the tiny peephole without being seen, ready to give the signal to attack the instant I saw Benji. Car doors opened, obscuring my vision, legs and baggage came into view, then—swish—two pairs of legs, one female, whisked by me in a blur before I could see any higher than the waist.

The lock in the room next door clicked, but we didn't know who it was. Was Benji in the room, or still in the car—had they switched cars on the way? Should we gamble it was him and rush in, or wait until we were sure? How *big* was the Moonie with him?

The silver Mustang moved slowly toward a parking spot, but I couldn't see who the driver was. Nearby Dr. Leof and his wife appeared confused.

"What are you doing, you idiot?" I heard him yell, waving his arms at his wife, who leapt from the car and stormed off. They were trying to tell us something—but we didn't have a clue what it was.

Lenny and Mr. Miller scrambled to the back door of our hotel room, pressing their ears against it to identify the voices in the adjacent room.

"I think I hear Benji," mumbled Lenny, but Mr. Miller disagreed. Minutes were ticking away and Benji—if it was him—might leave any second. What the hell were we supposed to do?

Finally, in a flash of desperate bravado, Dr. Leof came to the rescue. Storming up to our room in complete frustration, he pounded on the door with all his might, and yelled so loud that half the hotel could hear:

"What the hell are you doing in there? Benji's next door—get the hell out there and KIDNAP him!!"

As soon as Dr. Leof's words had registered, Simon and I charged out the front door, while Lenny and Gary grappled at the one connecting the two motel rooms.

"Okay, I'll open the door and you charge in!" shouted Gary.

"The hell," countered Lenny. "*You* open the door and *you* charge in!"

As the door was flung open Gary burst into the room and saw Benji and his mother standing by the bathroom sink, watering a bunch of flowers. The Moonie accompanying Benji was not in the room. Gary charged, grabbing Benji in a choke hold and pulling back with all his strength—but as he did he squeezed Mrs. Miller up against the sink. She shrieked and tumbled into the bathtub, flowers covering her like a body ready for burial.

Lenny, Simon and Dr. Leof arrived and grabbed Benji from the front. His arms flailed to escape and his eyes registered what Dr. Leof later called the "most terrifying blank expression I have ever seen". Then momentarily Benji noticed Simon, and for an eerie second he seemed to return to the Benji of old. He stopped, as in a freeze-frame of a movie, and said: "Hi Simon—what are you doing here?"

But an instant later his eyes were distant again, and he was fighting to escape as though all of us—including his parents—were total strangers. I raced outside to see what had happened to the escort Moonie.

To my horror, I saw him backing the Mustang out of its parking spot unimpeded and preparing to take off for help.

Somehow Dr. G. had dozed off and neglected to cut off the Moonie vehicle.

Racing toward the car, I pulled at the passenger door handle to no avail, then scrambled atop the hood—freezing before the windshield and staring into the Moonie's eyes as he tried to get the car in gear.

"No-o-o!" I shouted, scrambling off the hood and diving for the door handle, praying it might be unlocked. My fingers gripped the metal, the door swung open and I flung myself into the Moonie's lap, shouting:

"Wait! Wait! We just want to talk to Benji. Please listen! We have deportation papers taken out on Benji, but we don't want to use them—we just want to talk..." I rambled, bluffing wildly. I was running out of steam, when Dr. G. suddenly swung into action.

Peeling his car out of its parking spot with squealing tires, he tore toward us, terrifying us and hotel guests gaping at the scene. At the last second he screeched to a stop, inches from the Moonie's Mustang, then slammed his door and stormed toward us.

"FBI!" he snarled, shoving his open wallet briefly through the window and grabbing the Moonie by the shirt. "Out of the car, punk!" The Moonie froze, and I slapped at Dr. G's arm and yelled in spontaneous histrionics:

"Hold it! We had a deal...you said there'd be no trouble if he let us see Benji peacefully. Don't double-cross us!"

It was a third-rate performance, but enough to confuse the Moonie, and he jerked his eyes from one of us to the other, shouting: "What's going on—what's happening?" His voice was strained and his manner frantic—but as I looked into his eyes they seemed completely dead.

Back in the room, Benji was struggling to escape, though clearly shocked by the presence of his haggard father and friends in the kidnapping. Finally, Lenny rushed out to get me, hoping one more familiar face might break his resistance completely.

I abandoned my play acting with Dr. G. and ran into the room to deal with Benji. I couldn't; as soon as I looked into his vacant, alien eyes I burst into tears.

"Damn you, Benji..." I sputtered. "We've spent ten thousand dollars and six weeks' time to get out here and talk to you...just *talk* to you! Just...just...get out of here!"

Somehow that seemed to work. Moved by my tears and those of his parents, Benji became subdued for a moment; we took advantage of the calm to pin his arms and rush him out the door.

As we stepped out into the light, half carrying Benji, hotel guests peered down from every balcony at the spectacle—while Dr. Leof, Dr. G. and Dr. F. moved casually about reassuring them with "I'm a psychiatrist...it's only a patient...please don't worry"; or "FBI!...shut up and say nothing!"

In the confusion, the other Moonie raced off in the Mustang for help, but we paid no attention. Dr. M. pulled in with the getaway car; its doors opened. I fell in backward, pulling Benji by the neck, and Simon fell in on top of him, shouting: "Please Benji—*please!*"

Only a tangle of legs still protruded through the car door. Gary stuffed them in like so many sticks of lumber and jumped in himself; at last, the car squealed and lurched out of the parking lot and onto the nearby highway.

"Jesus...that was close!" I gasped, easing my stranglehold on Benji, only to realize that it was no longer needed. Our friend was sitting bolt upright, eyes riveted to the floor in a trance-like state he would maintain for more than 24 hours—and nothing we would say would draw him out. We tore down the highway in complete silence, wondering what we were going to do next.

Forty-five minutes later we were safely parked in the underground garage of our hotel in Berkeley, triumphant grins stretched across our sweating faces. Benji was still in a trance as we pulled him from the car.

Halfway to the stairs he kneeled to tie his shoelace, then made a break for it. We grabbed him, pinned his arms apologetically, then carried and shoved him up three flights of back stairs and down the hotel corridor. With a collective sigh, we hauled him into our own room, then piled tables and chairs against the door.

Bad news was waiting. Mr. Miller was already back at the hotel in a room down the hall, but his wife—who suffered from high blood pressure—was very faint. He was in his room waiting for a doctor, but had phoned to give us worse tidings: our own hotel room was registered in his name, and could probably be traced by anyone who called.

I rushed downstairs to the main lobby, then casually walked up to the middle-aged woman plumped at the reception counter.

She was a stern-looking Scottish matron, and she glared at me as I approached in my clearly dishevelled condition.

"Uhhh...I hate to ask you this..." I stumbled, "but could we change the registered name on our hotel room—fast!"

"And *why-y-y?*" she demanded, looking me dead in the eyes.

I had no choice. Swallowing, I asked her if she had ever heard of Rev. Moon.

"That bastar-r-rd!" she replied in a cold Scottish brogue. "Someone should put a *bullettt* between his blades!"

"Whew," I sighed, spilling my story quickly and begging her help. In moments, she agreed, flashing a sympathetic smile; then she raised her finger to deliver a piece of motherly advice:

"There's just one thing I've been meaning to tell you ever since you checked in a few days ago...

"I've been in the hotel business for twenty years...but I've never seen guests more *susss-picious* than the lot of you—whispering and plotting and coming and going all night long. I had a mind to call the police myself last night—not because I suspected you of anything...you're much too *harrrmless* looking for that—but because I worried you might be in some kind of trouble yourrselves!"

Some time later we had settled down in the hotel room and were trying to break through Benji's silence. His father came by to talk with him but the attempt was futile: Benji gazed by Mr. Miller as though he were a stick of furniture.

When the usually jovial father abandoned his efforts and returned to his ailing wife, there were tears streaming down his face. Benji's sister Debbie had met a similar fate, crying "Benji—what's wrong...BENJI!" to the brother she hadn't seen in a year. But Benji would not so much as look up to acknowledge her.

The only momentarily brightening words had come from Mazzoni, who had phoned the room from somewhere to tell us he was "proud...you need some polish, but it was a great first kidnapping!...You guys have got a real future."

Now I was reading Benji some material on Rev. Moon's financial interests, in hope that some of the information might get through the screen of silence around him. We were steadying ourselves for a long night—when unexpectedly the phone rang. It was the Scottish woman at the desk.

"Come down quickly," she growled in a low voice. "It's very important that I see you."

Gary hurried down to the reception desk where the woman was nervously waiting. "The police just called," she told Gary softly. "They wanted to know if I had a Mr. Miller on my books—but I told them I didn't give out that information over the phone. "They said they'd be coming over soon and check it themselves..."

"Whee-eew!" Gary whistled, trying to figure out our next step. "Did they say when they'd be ov-"

He never finished the sentence: the woman had gone stiff as a board. "My God," she whispered, the blood draining from her face.

"They're standing right behind you *now*."

8

Our new hide-out was a small cottage with a tiny blue bedroom that served as Benji's cell. Crowded quarters, but far more spacious than the real police cell we had all so narrowly escaped.

Only fifteen minutes earlier we'd been sitting comfortably in our Berkeley hotel room when Gary had rushed in with word that the police and Moonies were searching the building; somehow they had pinpointed our hotel. The police had been only inches from Gary, but had failed to spot him as one of the kidnappers. He had slipped between the two officers with a whispered "excuse me", then sauntered across the lobby just as police and Moonies began flooding the hotel.

Turning down the main corridor, Gary had raced back to our room. In seconds we had grabbed Benji again and trundled him down the back stairs like a sack of potatoes. We crowded into our car and sped out of the garage; by the time we reached the street, the police were searching our room.

Luckily Dr. M. lived only a few blocks away, and we were at his house in minutes. It was cramped: the small cell-like room for Benji and a double living room for the rest of us, furnished with the sparse accoutrements of a counter-culture doctor. Some beat up furniture. An expensive stereo. A hammock. The odd stethoscope lying about. A sign on the front door read: "To be sure of hitting the target—shoot first, and whatever you hit—call the target."

Immediately upon arriving, we began barricading the windows and stripping Benji's room of sharp or pointed objects such as bottles and pencils. Many Moonies have been taught that it is better to die than to be deprogrammed; some have been given razor blades with instructions on how to attempt suicide, down to the precise angle at which to slash their wrists.

"Slash across for the hospital, down for death" was their chilling "razor blade rule", and several members had used it in the past. We didn't know if Benji had learned the "technique"—but looking at him, we weren't going to take the chance.

Our friend's appearance was appalling. Emaciated and pale, the once gregarious Benji sat with his eyes bolted to the floor, their black pupils twice normal size. He had gone into some kind of trance to avoid speaking to us, mutely chanting what we later discovered was: *"Glory to Heaven. Peace on Earth. Get me out to serve whole purpose."*

"Benji!" we shouted again and again in complete frustration, as though shouting at someone who was out of earshot. "What are you doing—why don't you talk to us? All we want to do is discuss this thing with you—make sure you know what you're doing...Benji—this is *crazy*...why won't you just *talk* about it?"

It was like speaking to a corpse. Hour after hour he sat as rigid as a block of stone, back erect, gazing into space as though we were not even present. His transmogrification was shocking and utterly incomprehensible; for the first time since the strange odyssey had begun, all of us knew we had done the right thing in grabbing our friend. And we also knew that we needed a "deprogrammer", if we were ever going to reach him again.

For the rest of the evening, we kept at least one person talking with him at all times, to no avail. At eleven p.m. Benji silently turned over and dropped off to sleep. We laid a blanket over him, turned off his light and called Montreal to bring our anxious friends up to date. Following some discussion, we called Neil Maxwell and several other San Francisco contacts; after weeks of delaying the decision, we asked them to help us find a deprogrammer.

Soon afterwards, we settled down to guard duty and flicked on the television for diversion. By a startling coincidence the screen was filled with the face of Sun Myung Moon, who had rented a half hour of TV time to "talk to America". For the next thirty minutes, Moon's shrill voice and karate-chop gesticulations filled our little outpost in a frightening display. It included a tape of a $1 million firework show the Moonies had sponsored in Washington, and a passionate appeal by Moon himself for God to "Bless America" in the holy war against the communist devil.

"MAN-SEI!!" shrieked 1500 Moonies, dropping to their knees before Moon and saluting skyward with clenched fists that seemed to come from a single body. "VICTORY FOR FATHER!"

We spent the night in a watchful vigil, alternating sentry posts from Benji's room to the front and back windows of the house—though there was little we could have done had the police or Moonies arrived. As darkness blanketed the city, the ordinary noises of night began to seem like enemy activity: the rustle of trees and windows sounded like prowling strangers, the barking of neighbourhood dogs was mistaken for approaching bloodhounds. Even the wail of the occasional ambulance convinced us that a full-scale police dragnet was hunting us in the streets.

Despite our paranoia, one sound still amused us: Benji's buzz-saw snoring—the only thing about him that hadn't changed. It reverberated through the tiny house all night long, like an eerie musical score.

The still night was fertile ground for moral unrest too, providing the chance to ponder and discuss our strange venture. We had run on instinct all the way through the kidnapping, and now that it was over, many thoughts raced through our minds. Had it made any sense to kidnap Benji? It was obvious he did not want anything to do with us. But was the person in the next room really Benji—and what would the old Benji have to say? Would we ever see him again to find out?

What of the deprogrammer? Were we right to call one in, and what would he be like, if he ever showed up? One thing we were all agreed upon: regardless of what the deprogrammer had to say, we would not keep Benji captive indefinitely. If he didn't start talking in the next couple of days, we would have to let him go—whatever the consequences.

And what would happen if we were caught? There were more than 40 people involved in planning the kidnapping—how would they ever bring us all to trial? "Hell of a good story!" I scribbled into my notebook, alongside the tangled thoughts of the night's writing; it was the newsman in me, returning for the first time in a long while...

Several hours and cups of coffee later, morning peeked through our tightly shuttered windows. All of us were haggard and disconsolate, and I decided to chance calling the Berkeley hotel to speak with Benji's father for advice; we had had no word from him since our flight from the hotel. The phone rang several times. When Mr. Miller finally answered, he was nervous and brief:

"Josh...I can't talk...the police are outside our door," he whispered. "We seem to be under arrest."

For Charlie Miller and his family, events had moved quickly from the harrowing to the horrid. The kidnapping had been the most distressing moment of Charlie's life: his son Benji, virtually unrecognizable behind the strangely flat gaze that failed to respond to his own family; his wife Libby crying as the "boys" had grabbed Benji; himself so nervous he could not even bear to look, let alone help subdue his son. When the "boys" had finally stuffed his son's flailing body into the getaway car, Charlie had held his wife in his arms as she cried for them to let Benji go; then he had hustled her and his daughter Debbie into another vehicle and careened away from the hotel.

The drive had been a nightmare; watching for police, worrying about Benji, listening dumbstruck to his wife's description of her airport encounter with her son. "It wasn't Benji, Charlie, it wasn't him at all. He's so pale and skinny you could die...and his eyes!...What have they done to him?!"

Then the news that the Moonie accompanying Benji was his nephew; Charlie hadn't seen the boy since he'd left home three years earlier. A police car passed and Charlie winced at the sight for the first time in his life. Beside him, he could see that Libby was pale, her blood pressure acting up despite her stoic efforts.

At the Berkeley hotel, matters were even worse. The brief encounter with his son seemed to Charlie to be the nadir of his existence. He had fled back to look after his wife, more convinced than ever that Benji was lost.

Soon after, he had heard a commotion in the hotel corridor—as we rushed by with Benji—but he had hesitated to look out for fear it was the authorities; then, even as he could hear our receding footsteps, the police had come lumbering up the front stairs to pound on his door.

"Mr. Miller...Sergeant Sullivan, San Francisco Police."

The officer was a stocky, florid man, with a puffed face and a large pot belly: he wanted to know where Benji was.

"I haven't got the faintest idea," said Mr. Miller to the skeptical officer, as the two paunchy middle-aged men squared off against each other. The policeman was demanding, obviously uncomfortable with his task. He shrugged nervously and told Charlie:

"I hate doing this, Mr. Miller...I have a wife and children at home too, you know."

Eventually, Sergeant Sullivan had confined them to their room, indicating that formal kidnapping charges would soon be brought. He told the Millers to "get smart" and tell him what had happened by morning. Before leaving, Sullivan had pointed suspiciously at Mr. Miller's file, crammed with information on the Moonies; it was labelled "BBB"—an acronym for "Bring Back Benji".

"What do the letters stand for, Mr. Miller?" asked the sergeant.

"Nothing..." replied Charlie. "J...just scribbling."

"Hmmm..." said Sullivan, with a whimsical smile. Then he stuffed the file into his own dossier; it was labelled "MM"—short for "Missing Moonie".

When Sullivan left, no one in the family could sleep, despite their complete exhaustion. Mother and daughter lay awake on the bed the entire night, convinced they would soon be arrested; nearby, Charlie sprawled flat on his belly by the window. All night long he peered out the curtains at three police cars parked outside, pondering the unimaginable circumstances that had so changed his life. His only hope was the "boys", and the chance that they would somehow find a way to reach his son.

At nine a.m.—shortly after our call—there was a sharp knock at the hotel room door. Charlie opened it cautiously, expecting to see the police with a warrant for his arrest. It was a thin young man in a suit, a lawyer named Larry Shapiro sent by Dr. Leof to look after the Millers. He had bad news: the Moonies were assembling in the hotel lobby to hold a press conference about the kidnapping; a lawyer for the Unification Church had declared that if Benji were not back within 24 hours he would go to the FBI.

Within minutes, the Millers were following the young lawyer out of the hotel. As they moved through the main lobby, the Moonie lawyer was already giving a statement to the assembled news media; flashbulbs clicked and reporters clustered around the Millers as they moved briskly through the throng, refusing to make any comment. Outside, they scrambled into the back of the lawyer's car and drove quickly away; but several Moonies rushed to three waiting vans and trailed them down the street like a strange parade.

A hectic fifteen minute car ride later, the Millers arrived at the lawyer's office, with no sign of the Moonie vehicles behind them. Shortly afterwards, as they were sipping coffee, another young law partner stepped into the office, bewildered. "There are some pretty strange-looking people outside the office," he said innocently, still unaware of his partner's peculiar new case. "They look like Moonies...what the heck do you think they want?"

There was a rap at the window. A group of short-haired young men were standing outside, holding trays of coffee and cake and signalling for the lawyer to open the window. Behind them, several other youngsters dressed in white were busy sweeping the law firm's patio, in a scene reminiscent of a Fellini film.

"Jesus Christ!" exclaimed the lawyer, and seconds later he and his partner were assisting the distraught Millers downstairs to the garage. They split up into two cars. One of the lawyers drove out of the garage as a decoy, the other followed with the Millers several minutes later. The ploy was partly successful. When Charlie looked out the back window minutes afterward, only one van was still in pursuit.

The next ten minutes was a high speed chase, the Millers' car swerving around corners and down back streets in an attempt to shake the remaining van. It was no use. As they sped out onto the entranceway of the busy Golden Gate Bridge, the Moonies were still close behind. Then, as they approached the bridge's toll booth, the Moonies committed a blunder, pulling into one of the pay tolls ahead of the car they were tailing. The lawyer in the Miller's car acted quickly.

"Excuse me...This is an emergency!" he told the elderly guard at the toll booth window, as the Moonie van was forced ahead onto the bridge by heavy traffic. Pulling out every identification card he could muster, the lawyer convinced the guard to stop the traffic and let him turn around. The old man emerged reluctantly from his booth and began to bring four lanes of traffic to a halt.

Once traffic had been stopped, the young lawyer drove his car over the frozen car-jam to the other side of the highway—only to see the Moonies' van heading back their way.

The Moonies had seen their mistake, and somehow managed to wheel their vehicle around on the bridge. The lawyer thought quickly. He peeled his car back across the four lanes of stalled vehicles, then charged by the startled guard and through the toll booth—right by the Moonie vehicle, which was mired in frozen traffic going the other way.

"Whew...that was pretty good if I say so myself," said the slightly smug voice of the attorney, as he pressed the gas pedal to the floor. In the back seat, Mrs. Miller's face was pale, her eyes closed, still tensed for the sound of crunching metal. Up in the passenger seat, Charlie Miller let out a long whistling breath and smiled broadly. He never saw the Moonies again.

Back at Dr. M's place, tension was growing. Keith had shown up at the hide-out with copies of morning newspapers carrying our "story". "MOONIE SNATCHED" said one headline in the San Francisco Examiner. "THE CASE OF THE DISAPPEARING MOONIE" read another in the Oakland Tribune, with a front page box highlighting an inside story, that began:

"The Canadian parents of a 27-year-old man who joined the controversial Unification Church have spirited him away in hope that he can be deprogrammed, according to lawyers for the church."

But the "hope" that the article referred to was quickly fading for those who had done the "spiriting away". Benji had just woken up after a long night's sleep, as silent and unresponsive as the evening before. Lenny was still trying to get through to him when Charlie Miller phoned with news of their narrow escape.

After some discussion, all agreed that the Millers should not risk coming to the hide-out; the police or the Moonies might still have them under surveillance. As well, Mrs. Miller's blood pressure was still high and she might require medical attention. She was more than willing to join us in hiding, but overall it seemed wisest to go through the deprogramming without their help. We were far from certain a deprogramming would even take place: Maxwell still had not found a deprogrammer, and it looked more and more likely the police would find us first.

Blunders seemed to be following us as closely as our own shadows. When we scrambled from the Berkeley hotel room the night before, I stupidly left a notebook behind; it contained phone numbers of everyone who had helped us, including Dr. M. The police had seized the notebook, and in case they needed more clues, Simon had left his camera behind with convenient souvenir photos of all of us inside.

The Moonies were also reacting with unusual urgency. Not only had they organized the press campaign, but they had assigned carloads of Moonies to trail almost every known anti-cult figure in the city. Mose Durst himself, the head of the California Church, had trailed Neil Maxwell to the grocery that morning.

The unusually strong response seemed partly due to Benji's value: he had money, brains and education. The Moonies' dragnet also appeared to be their first response to the recent California Court decision ruling that parents of adult cult members had no right to custody of their children.

This made it clear for the first time that parents who abducted Moonies were no different from other kidnappers; it was an undeniable, serious criminal offence. According to several lawyers we consulted by phone. the Moonies were looking for a good test case, and we were it; if caught and convicted, we could face ten years in jail.

We decided to inform Benji of our increasingly critical dilemma. He was still mute, coming out of his trance-like state only momentarily to eat his meals; then, mysteriously obeying some Moonie ritual of sharing, he would divide his food into equal portions and pass it silently out to us.

We told him of his parents' difficulties with the police and his mother's precarious health. He had no visible emotional response, but it obviously had some effect because he broke his self-imposed silence for the first time to make a brief, passionless declaration.

"Let me go..." Benji said in a slow monotone, as his head pivoted slowly upwards to look at us for the first time. His eyes, charcoal black from the size of his pupils, gazed slightly by me. "There won't be any kidnap charges."

Benji's head pivoted downwards again, and he would say nothing more. There was no way to know if he meant what he said, and even if he did he might change his mind once he was free. Other Moonies had launched suits against parents and friends for millions of dollars; there was no reason to believe Benji would act differently—especially after another long session at Boonville. In any event, the question of "clemency" hardly mattered. After coming this far, we weren't going to give up without a fight. And if nothing else, we had the constant support of a collection of intimate strangers like Keith to bolster our sagging spirits.

Keith had become our virtual lifeline with the world beyond the shuttered windows. His absence from the kidnapping had proved to be a blessing in disguise; it meant that no one had seen him take part in the crime. In the morning, Keith would saunter out of the house and buy us a case of Coors beer, which he quaffed continuously from breakfast onwards. He brought us our food as well, mainly corn-stuffed enchilada bombshells from a nearby taco factory that kept us sated for hours at a time.

Beer in one hand, tamale in the other, the hulking woodsman would keep our morale afloat for hours on end with tales of Loafer's Glory and his incomparable "grandpappy"—a mountain man of such repute that: "S'help me if the willow trees themselves didn't bend down and touch his head whenever he walked through the forest."

Dr. M. had also proved a welcome, if less heroic, addition to our team. The hippie doctor played the chicken heart's role with a black humour that warmed us, musing on the liklihood of good weed and conjugal visits if he ended his career in prison.

Dr. Leof was miles away, but his invisible hand was always

close by, arranging legal assistance, providing care for the Millers, and making contingency plans for another hide-out and getaway car should something go amiss. Maxwell was ever in touch as well, keeping us abreast of his search for a deprogrammer, and lawyers, San Francisco friends, and ex-cult members all forwarded messages that warmed our spirits. Montreal friends called frequently too, running up a long distance bill that topped $1000. Even if nothing was going right, no deprogrammer had yet been found, and Benji was miles away—Lenny, Simon, Gary and I felt closer to home than ever.

At three p.m. that day we found a deprogrammer. He was Ford Greene, an ex-Moonie who had gone into Boonville to retrieve his sister, only to succumb himself. After eight mindless months as a Moonie, he had somehow convinced himself to leave, painfully "unbrainwashing" himself as he put it, over nearly a year's time.

For the past two years, Ford had been a deprogrammer, earning himself a reputation as one of the most effective on the West Coast. He credited himself with 38 deprogrammings, and only two failures, both of whom escaped during the deprogramming. He and his parents faced a $5.2 million lawsuit for allegedly trying to deprogram Ford's sister. During the session she slashed her wrist with a shard of glass, sideways, and was rushed to hospital where the Moonies recovered her. Today she is treated as a virtual saint in Church propaganda.

Ford's success rate had not gone unnoticed by the Moonies. They identified him as the "special servant of Satan", a mindless psychopath who roamed the streets looking to steal the souls of idealistic youth. To them he was evil incarnate, a terrifying spectre with no control over even his own "ravaged" mind. I had talked to him over the phone, and he certainly sounded like a tough customer.

"If you want me, I have to be in complete charge," he stated bluntly in a voice that singed my ear. "If anyone else interferes, I leave."

Ford told me it would cost $750 for the deprogramming, regardless of how long it took, including follow up advice afterwards. It seemed a lot—but there wasn't much choice, and Neil Maxwell recommended him highly; we agreed to his terms. Then we sat down to continue our anxious vigil, waiting to see who would get there first—the deprogrammer or the police.

By five p.m. we were all at our nerves' ends. Even Keith was prowling to the window like a cat at every sound. I was in the bedroom vainly talking to Benji, while Simon and Lenny snoozed in the parlour. Suddenly there were three heavy, measured knocks at the front door; Keith leapt to the window and peeked out.

"It's a tall dude, but I can't see who," Keith whispered, in his southern twang. "Get ready...I'm gonna let him in."

Awakening from sleep, Lenny pulled himself up and waited to jump. He hoped for the deprogrammer and feared the Moonies—but he wasn't ready for what walked in. As the door cracked open, a gaunt six foot-three figure leaned its head around and peered in.

His face was pale as chalk, with fresh scars, raw stitches, and a black patch over one eye. The other eye stared out unblinking, burning into Lenny's forehead, while the mouth leered and whispered: "Ford Greene."

Lenny hardly heard the words. Exhausted and just waking up, he thought he was dreaming; he squinted into the open doorway and felt as if a cold wind were blowing over his whole body:

"My God," he said to himself. "It *is* the devil."

9

"*Love* me, Benji...Love Satan."

Ford Greene had draped his arm round Benji's shoulders, pressed his forehead and nose firmly against his, and now was peering unblinking into Benji's eyes, hissing:

"Why can't you love even me...Satan...if you're really such a *loving* person."

Benji sat with back erect, eyes expressionless, hands folded in his lap like a nun: a picture of serenity, except for a red face, tightly flexed muscles and a vein in his forehead that throbbed visibly. The vein was taut as a spring, indicating that for the first time in 24 hours, Benji was feeling some emotion, even if it was fear.

Benji's deprogramming had begun, and it seemed to be a virtual exorcism at the hands of the "special servant of Satan".

Ford Greene looked the part. His face was freshly scarred from a recent car accident and his black patch was now removed, revealing a contused and grisly eye that was even more unnerving. When he stood, his gaunt body hovered over Benji like a macabre scarecrow.

"He's not thinking, not feeling," Ford had warned us minutes earlier. "He's dead. Before I can make him talk, I've got to make him feel *something*...and fear is the primal feeling."

"*Stamp out Satan. Stamp out Satan. Stamp out Satan*" his silent opponent chanted to himself, bracing for battle, as we found out later.

Ford had laid his cards squarely on the table upon entering the bedroom where I sat with Benji. He told him: *"You believe that Moon is the Messiah and that the rest of the world—especially me—is purely Satanic.*

"I believe that Moon is a fraud, Satan doesn't exist and you have been brainwashed. Only one of us can be right, Benji...and we're here to find out who."

Now he stood in front of Benji, challenging his silence with a torrent of words, taunting him to speak.

"You're a zombie, a robot," he announced to the lifeless figure. "Your eyes are vacant, your veins are sticking out, your pupils are dilated and your skin is pale...You're dead man...they've got you good," Ford concluded, flashing a bold smile before he turned to leave the room. "But don't worry, I'm here to give you a life transfusion...a soul injection!

"And I'm going to stay as long as it takes to get you to talk—whether that's a day, a month...or a year."

The door closed behind him and I joined Benji in silence. It had been a grotesque show, and I squirmed in my seat, fumbling to say something to disassociate myself from it.

"I...uhh...well...he's kind of heavy...but I think he's okay," I stammered, my eyes swinging from the doorway to Benji's face. For the first time since the kidnapping, he seemed to hear me, and I thought I saw a smile flicker across his face.

Exorcist: there seemed to be no other word for Ford and the job he did. The godson of former U.S. Congressman James Buckley, Ford was bright and articulate, intense and loving, his presence so electric his words crackled when he spoke.

A mane of greasy brown hair hung from the peak of his tall, thin frame and his eyes stared out hypnotically, gripping you like pincers; then, unexpectedly, the pressure was gone, dissolving into an incandescent smile and a lusty, throaty laugh.

Part-time auto mechanic, part-time antique dealer, and sometime deprogrammer, Ford had a primal sense of power: it seemed incredible that he could have fallen into the

Moonies. Yet for months he had been trapped in the cult, until—as though watching himself through a window from outside—he had seen his mind degenerate, reducing in scope and articulation, slowly changing into "something I would once have despised".

By sheer will, Ford had pulled himself out of Boonville and spent eleven months painfully deprogramming himself, still believing that Moon was the Messiah though his mind knew the truth. He read, studied and talked to ex-members, sleeping three months with the light on for fear of Satan, alternating from one reality to the other like a rock skipping across water, until at last the nightmare had ended and he had returned to his former self.

Since then he had been helping others to do less painfully what he had done to himself. He was one of the best.

Minutes after he arrived, Ford tightened "security". Benji's room was stripped of light bulbs and his drinking cup was replaced with a plastic bottle; the door to the room was also removed and furniture stacked against the window. Beer was banned from the room in deference to Benji's beliefs.

Arriving with Ford was Virginia, a recent ex-Moonie and friend of Benji who had heard of the deprogramming from Maxwell. She wanted to help, though she was as different from Ford as silk from steel.

A schoolteacher brimming with openness and trust, Virginia had been attracted to the Moonies with the false promise of work in an "alternative school". The young woman had gone to Boonville for what she thought was a "training seminar" for her new job, but had been quickly caught in the camp's psychological web, and given up work to join the Moonies. The journey had ended a year later on a flower-selling team working more than 20 hours a day, her legs scarred by infection, her mind by fear.

"Hi Benji!" she bubbled, bounding into the bedroom like a summer breeze only seconds after Ford's grim presence had left. "It's really GREAT to see you."

The stiff figure she addressed didn't blink, but Virginia was undaunted.

"Come on Benji...you know me. I'm Virginia. We sold flowers together, chanted and sang with each other...*shared* with each other. Benji. C'mon Benji...TALK to me," she threatened, "...or I'll tickle you."

Virginia had the verve of a chipmunk and the smile of an angel. After 24 hours of silence and Ford's intense attack, she was more than Benji could handle. Slowly, mechanically, his gaze pivoted upwards. When his eyes met hers, a dull string of words came reluctantly from his mouth.

"I don't want to talk about it Virginia. Not here...not now. I won't talk."

From that point on, he never stopped talking. Like a shy child opening to a stranger, Benji began to respond to Virginia, nodding his head at first, then grunting out terse sentences as if by rote.

"Father says Satan works best through those you know and trust. Father says we must resist...we have to combine heart and intellect. That's the only way to serve God."

Benji kept on responding hesitantly even when Ford returned to the room. Ford was different now, his face gentler, his eyes still intent. He had slipped quietly into a corner of the room to interject a question here, a comment there—until, crackling then igniting, like a fire spreading from edges to the core, Benji and Ford began to debate.

For a college graduate who had long scorned religion Benji now inhabited an alien world. Long sympathetic to socialism, he was now virulently anti-communist; always sensitive to women's rights, he was suddenly convinced of female inferiority; a gentle tolerant person with a good word for everyone, he now had contempt for anyone but Moonies.

Most surprisingly, the Jewish agnostic had become a zealot for a strange new religion. He talked of devils and spirits, serpents and Messiahs, Evil and Good; there were no shades of gray in his black and white world.

Mankind lived in darkness, consumed, hateful and doomed, its only hope the burning sun of the Unification Church, last bastion of purity on the face of the earth. At the top of his universe was Sun Myung Moon, leading the way to an "ideal world" where people would stop thinking about "self" and start serving "others".

The aims sounded noble, but the route had taken a horrible wrong turn.

According to the Principle which ruled his life like an iron fist, nothing mattered in life but utter devotion to Father Moon: every hour, every minute, every second spent otherwise—spacing out, reading or thinking—was a waste of God's time, not just a waste of the moment, but a betrayal of every moment that had led up to it and every one that might be born of it.

Unification Church members were in the very crucible of history. Every instant was of unthinkable magnitude. To pause, doubt or question was not just to be heretic, but to deliberately fling a crowbar into the rolling wheel of history at a crucial moment. Even to consider leaving the movement was the greatest sin possible, more horrible than death. One could only obey, follow Father wherever his wisdom led. If Satan invaded in the guise of doubt or unproductive thought, Benji's only duty was to burn it from his consciousness by chanting "Stamp out Satan" over and over again, until the evil had been cauterized and his mind was once again clean to serve Father. Even if it meant death, Benji hoped to have the strength to serve, even in the face of the Holy War that Father had prophesied in which one-third of the world might die: "Nothing is better than to die in service," said Father.

Ford's task was to penetrate this mental armor, in a psychological duel with no quarter given. Standing, kneeling, pacing and whirling, Ford swept to the attack, his gestures lurching yet graceful, like the thoughts they punctuated.

Against him was a different Benji from the one we had seen in the past 24 hours: a serious young student, with unblinking eyes and rigid posture but talking now, as determined as a Talmudic scholar to show "Satan's servant" the error of his ways.

Stamp out Satan. Stamp out Satan. BE POSITIVE.

It began slowly with soft questions by Ford and more rote answers by Benji from the Divine Principle.

"Man's Mission is to serve God...According to principle we can only become perfect children by following God's standard under Father."

"No Benji...that's what *they* told you. I want to know what *you* think."

Relentlessly, Ford's questions moved on, probing and grinding at Benji's inconsistencies till the questions were like blows and Benji scurried to retreat.

"If Satan was really there first, why did he need Adam? How could Adam eat the apple if Satan wasn't there yet?"

They sounded like two priests on a mountaintop: none of us could understand a word they were saying. Two logical minds were battling on completely illogical terrain; at times Ford sounded crazier than Benji and we feared we had made a mistake in calling him in—until slowly we would glimpse the logic of his plan.

Pausing after each question with a pregnant "Benn-ji" that hung in the silence, Ford waited for Benji to answer, then stabbed at the web of illogic surrounding his adversary.

"How can you believe in unconditional *love*...and *hate* those who don't believe?"

"How is selling flowers to a penniless old woman helping to save the world from selfishness? It's just Satan's money, isn't it Benji...isn't that what they told you?...It's okay to tell her that the money goes to ghetto children and take her last dollar—because the *poorer* she is...the bigger the *blessing* will be.

"You think you're learning to love...but actually you're learning to hate! Hate sex, hate your family, hate yourself...all in the name of loving. What kind of *love* is that?

"THINK Benji! Use your mind again—that's what it's for. There's nothing Satanic about asking questions and having doubts."

Statistics on Moon's wealth; reports on political links; portions of the Church's philosophy that Benji was not due to hear for months; testimony after testimony of ex-members attacking the Church, many of them by former high-ups who had been close to "Father": Ford forced Benji to confront the philosophy he had swallowed, and its final implications.

"What wouldn't you do for Reverend Moon, Benji? What if evil wouldn't stop—what if it wouldn't let up, and Father ordered you to kill? If you'd lie and you'd cheat for him, wouldn't you have to kill too, if he ordered you to..."

"Not necessarily," replied Benji hesitantly. "We're still human...I...I...could say no."

"No Benji, that's not what the Principle says," retorted Ford. "Doesn't Moon say 'You must walk upside down if I order you to'? Doesn't he say 'I am your brain'? Doesn't he say 'You must be prepared to fight and die for Korea'?

"What does it mean to disobey Moon, Benji?...You know the answer, but you're avoiding it," said Ford, and Benji's silence told us that he did.

"If you disobey Moon, you disobey God and follow Satan," spelled out Ford, enunciating each word slowly, "and you are condemned to eternal damnation for all time.

"Don't you see Benji?...There's no room for mistakes in a system of absolute good and evil."

"But...but that would mean we were just robots..." stammered Benji, his black eyes coming to life for the briefest moment.

"Exactly, Benji," answered Ford softly. *"Exactly."*

It was a painstaking process: unwinding the doctrine, unravelling the knots in Benji's mind, untwisting the half-truths that had seemed so logical at Boonville, where little sleep, less protein and no time alone had weakened him to the point where anything could slip in.

Like artifical respiration of the mind—trying to breathe life into a suffocating brain.

Benji fought more courageously than most Moonies, bringing a talented mind to the defence of endless contradictions, slipping out of Ford's traps with agility only to have Ford fight him back into the corner again.

"He's smart," Ford gasped, sweating, during his first break four hours later. "The smartest one I've ever gone against...the dumb ones are easy."

Then back into the ring again, with an encouraging slap on the back and a glass of water to carry the next round. Throughout, Virginia was there with him, a gentle counterpoint to Ford's intensity, finding an easy smile at the most difficult moments, corroborating Ford's information with her own painful experience.

"I know you're terrified of leaving the Church, Benji...so was I," said Virginia. "They told me I'd become evil and depraved and kill everyone I saw. All ex-members are supposed to be whores, perverts and murderers...but none of it's true. People are real good in the outside world, Benji.

"Don't be afraid of your feelings, Benji...Satan won't get you if you leave."

Outside the tiny blue room, the rest of us waited anxiously for news, like relatives at an intensive care unit. Gary and Simon knelt on the floor, wading through files of Moon material, searching for scraps that might be helpful to Ford; Lenny and I alternated shifts in Benji's room, making sure a familiar face was always present; Keith and Dr. M. buoyed our spirits, bringing us food and word of the outside world.

That night, all of us gathered in Benji's room for a pizza dinner, eight of us sitting around the lifeless figure who surveyed the warm chatter with a puzzled look. It was a calm in the storm; for a brief time it felt as though we were back in the real world again, just a gang of friends sharing pizza and cokes.

"Lots of food and sleep, I want him healthy...we're not the Moonies," Ford had said at the beginning, and Benji was asleep at ten p.m. As we brewed coffee and began guard duty, Ford curled up on the wooden floor beside Benji and fell instantly asleep. Again the house was silent, except for Benji's snore, rumbling through the tiny house as he wrestled with his pillow through the night. Outside, a full moon once again peered from the night sky. It was the first one since the Harvest Moon: the Hunter's Moon.

At 6:15 Benji awoke, his eyes less glassy, and began to scribble questions on a scrap of paper. They were strange questions, relating to obscure points in the Divine Principle, but it didn't matter: they were his first ones. Ford was excited; questions meant Benji's mind was beginning to work.

The morning went quickly as Benji's mind warmed up and he began to question his behavior with us in dry clinical terms.

Why had he deceived people when selling flowers and gathering converts? Why had he refused to spend more time with Marilyn and me during our first trip to California? Why had he agreed to suspend normal thinking processes and give up his judgment to Moon?

Simply posing these questions was heresy for a Moonie, so we wondered if Benji was "deprogrammed". Was this lifeless shell all that was left of our friend?

"Don't worry," smiled Ford. "When he's deprogrammed...you'll know. You won't have to ask."

Benji asked to see our documentation on Moon's wealth and political connections; then at his request everyone but me left the room, and he knelt to pray. Kneeling on the bed amongst piles of paper, Benji prostrated himself toward the east, cupped his head in his hands and asked "Father" to guide him. He spent fifteen minutes kneeling there in silence, as I sat quietly in the corner of the room suddenly aware of how far we still had to go.

When the prayer ended, Ford returned and the debate resumed, more heated than ever.

"If Moon isn't the Messiah," Benji asked, looking desperately at Ford, "what about the Principle? If Reverend Moon's love isn't unselfish...whose is?"

The question was the final blasphemy, and Benji's voice was desperate as he searched for something to keep his world afloat after months of immersion in the Moonies. He needed something to replace Moon before he made the final leap, but Ford only shook his head.

"I'm sorry...I'm not God," he replied. "I don't have the answer... I'm just telling you that *yours* is a lie."

Benji looked bereft, and he repeated the question despairingly to each of us.

"Benji!" I shouted in frustration. "If you're looking for unselfish love, look around you...

"Your mother, your father, your friends, following you across the continent...dozens of people back in Montreal, who've spent six weeks and fifteen thousand dollars to send us here...

"Your mother sick, both your parents facing kidnapping charges and us sitting around here now scared to death we may end up in jail...all that just to *talk* to you. That's love...and if you don't see it, I think you're blind!"

The phone rang: it was Dr. Leof calling for news. As I left the room to talk with him, Lenny replaced me; Ford was in full steam, sensing Benji weakening.

"I mean...if Moon is the Messiah, Benji, then all your friends are evil for trying to sway you from Moon, and the harder they try, the more evil they are..."

"But what if they aren't evil, Benji?" he demanded. "What then? That would mean that everything Moon said was a monstrous lie—and that would mean he wasn't the Messiah...and if you go back to obey him, doesn't that mean you're a mindless zombie...a whore and a robot?

"So Benji...which one is it going to be?" Ford concluded, lurching toward Benji with a scarecrow-like motion, his voice falling to a near whisper. "Only *you*...can make the decision."

Their eyes were locked on each other. Ford's hand held Benji's knee gently. The vein on Benji's forehead was throbbing. Then the silence was broken by a hoarse cry from Lenny.

"Benji...do you think *I'm* evil?"

Benji's eyes jerked to Lenny, as he started to give the only answer possible for a Moonie—but the word seemed to stick in his throat, and his face turned red and swollen.

"I'm *not* evil..." choked Lenny. "None of us are evil, Benji..."

Weeping, Lenny's face rested on Benji's knee.

Only Benji remained emotionless, paralysed between opposing forces. Images of his parents in jail, his friends kidnapping him...the concern and feeling of the last day flashed through his mind like a kaleidoscope. *They're supposed to be evil...How can it be? It's all so confusing...*

"I *love* you Benji...we all love you," said Lenny, looking into Benji's eyes.

Benji blinked.

Lenny hugged him tightly, sobbing, and slowly a tear moved down Benji's impassive cheek, then another, and another...until suddenly, Benji shuddered, then burst into a gut-wrenching sob; he grasped Lenny like a life preserver, and collapsed in his arms.

In the living room, people were idly chatting when they heard a high-pitched wail, like a new-born baby's first scream. The door to the bedroom opened and Ford walked briskly out, like a doctor, and told us: "Get in there fast...he needs you all."

As we rushed into the room, we saw Benji and Lenny wet and red-faced, locked in each other's arms, hugging and crying; the next thing we knew, Benji was crying our names and pulling us in too, as we toppled into a mess of arms, legs and tears, losing ourselves to an overwhelming sense of relief.

There were five of us lying in the strange tangle—all husky men locked in a body-jam on the narrow bed. It was several minutes before our crying subsided. Our eyes were bloodshot and our faces red, and as we looked at one another for the first time the craziness of the scene finally struck—sweeping from one of us to another in a raw current of laughter until even Benji was laughing through his tears. In the midst of this bedlam, Virginia appeared in the doorway, her smile lighting up the room like sunshine as she cried out with delight:

"Welcome home, Benji... Welcome home!"

The metamorphosis in Benji, when he had stopped crying, was immediate and startling. His face changed completely from the stark mask Ford had confronted twenty-one hours earlier. His eyes had expression, his pupils were no longer dilated and his smile was full and natural again. Virginia, who had spent five months in the Moonies with him, discovered for the first time that he had dimples when he smiled.

Benji's voice was different too, while his manner was loose and animated; he responded to Keith and Dr. M. as though meeting them for the first time—shaking their hands and hugging them warmly when they were "introduced". It was as though an entirely new person had stepped into his body. Yet as different as he was, he was nothing new to us, just the old Benji we had always known. It seemed an extraordinary miracle to have him back.

Keith sat scratching his head and telling Benji over and over: "I can't believe yer the same person as that zombie...I just can't believe it. You're not even weird at all...you're a real good guy! I just can't believe it."

For Benji himself, the change was almost unfathomable, as though his mind had snapped back from a world in which everything had been seen through a distorting prism; it would be weeks before he could even begin to put the experience into words.

"It's so confusing...impossible!" is all he could say in the moments after his "break". "I feel...like my mind was wrapped in an elastic band—and somebody just cut it off. The only way I could ever believe that something like this could happen to someone like me...is to have it happen. It's all so incredibly confusing..."

Less than an hour after the deprogramming had ended, Ford was on his way, hugging Benji warmly then vanishing into the day; Virginia stayed on to help Benji sort things out in the coming days. As the two of them talked quietly in the corner of the room, we called a delighted Dr. Leof, who raced off to tell the Millers the news.

Soon, we were transforming our tiny hide-out into a home again—replacing the doors and lightbulbs to the relief of a nervous Dr. M. We even opened the curtains and blinds, letting the sun stream in for the first time in more than two days. When everything was in its place, Benji sat down to call Montreal, where so many people were still waiting for news—wondering how the deprogramming was faring and if the police were at our door. The phone in Montreal rang only once before an anxious Mike Kropveld answered.

"Hello...Mike?"

"Yeah...who's this...BENJI!?"

"Uh huh," Benji replied, breaking into a laugh that rippled across 4000 miles of telephone wire. "Guess what?...I'm deprogrammed!"

The days that followed were a slow sigh of relief. We remained in hiding for two days more while our lawyers arranged things with police. Everyone was tired and needed the rest—particularly Benji, who slept almost around the clock, waking only occasionally to eat huge portions of spaghetti.

Some 36 hours after the deprogramming had ended, we left our hide-out for the first time in four days. It was the dead of night, and we piled into Dr. M's Volvo and drove clear across town to a tiny French restaurant, where we hurried Benji inside.

When his mother first saw him, she cried out with delight, rushing over to Benji and hugging him so hard he almost keeled over backwards, laughing. His father and sister were seconds behind, adding their bodies to the joyful family reunion. Then, as Keith proposed a hearty "mountain toast" and Mrs. Miller beamed under her son's warm embrace, Benji was welcomed back to "life" in a scene so poignant even the restaurant waiters had to wipe away their tears.

The next day, Benji emerged in public to clear up our legal

mess. Sergeant Sullivan was in charge of the operation, arranging for all of us to meet without fanfare at a nearby law office. As the rest of us waited outside, Sullivan interviewed Benji in private to establish that he was leaving California of his own accord. The interview was taped, at the demand of the Moonies, and Sullivan could not say anything official until filing his report, nonetheless, he congratulated Charlie warmly on "finding" his missing son.

Sullivan ordered us to stay in town another day, until the case was officially "complete". No one complained, for it gave us a chance to thank so many people who had helped us. The Leofs, the lawyers and the doctors; Maxwell, Virginia, Ford, Keith, Mazzoni and many others who had lent a hand stopped by our hotel room that final day to join the fun; and smack in the centre of the celebration was Benji himself, thanking the many people he had never met.

It took an early morning phone call from Sullivan to break up our party. The details of our case had all been worked out and we were free to leave San Francisco immediately; a terse police report to the "watch commander" had officially wrapped up our case.

> Previously reported as missing under suspicious circumstances by fellow members of the Unification Church of San Francisco Benjamin "Benji" Miller has been located. Detective Patrick Sullivan met with Benji for approximately 60 minutes...During the course of the meeting (held out of the presence of family members and friends) Benji convinced interviewing officers that he was in no way being held against his will...Mr. Miller indicated that although he didn't wish to go into his personal reasons for leaving the Holiday Inn so suddenly last Friday night, he was in no way forced, enticed or coerced to leave the Unification Church."

Within hours of Sullivan's call, we had packed our bags and were heading out to San Francisco airport. There were nine of us taking the return flight home, and we were trailed to the airport by an honour guard of pin-striped lawyers, tipsy doctors and a lumbering mountain man. They had bought us "California" sweatshirts and armloads of San Francisco's yard-long sourdough bread. We were a strange spectacle indeed as we clambered aboard the plane.

The cabin doors shut, the engines roared and we were in the air, waving an unseen goodbye to the motley crew we left behind. When we arrived in Montreal, 25 more of Benji's friends were waiting to make the celebration complete.

Part II

10

As dramatic as Benji's deprogramming was it raised more questions than it answered in the months ahead. How had a bright college-educated agnostic come to believe that his family and friends were agents of Satan? How had he been convinced that a wealthy wheeler-dealer from Korea was the Messiah who would save the World? And most frightening, how was he—and thousands of others like him—transformed into a virtual automaton, with little apparent connection to his former self?

Can cults like the Unification Church be shrugged off as "surrogate mental hospitals for borderline psychotics", as our fellow kidnapper, Dr. Leof, believed when I first met him in San Francisco? Or are they more—and if so, what can they teach us about the human mind?

For close to a year, I have extensively interviewed Benji and other ex-moonies, talked with authorities in psychiatry, and read much of the literature available, in an attempt to understand the indoctrination process of the Unification Church. This research has convinced me that Boonville's techniques have an incredible inner logic; one that moves through the human psyche like the knife of a surgeon: a step-by-step process that tears apart the fabric of the recruit's reality, then eases him slowly into the new.

Much of the trail of this psychological scalpel can be traced with the help of several books published in the early 1960's investigating Korean and Chinese "brainwashing" techniques. Some of it can also be seen through the work of a handful of psychiatrists studying modern cult techniques—notably Dr. John Clark and Dr. Margaret Thaler Singer.

However, a full understanding, of this harrowing indoctrination process can only begin with the experience of those who have been through it—like Benji.

Benji's voyage began at the house on Washington Steet. He had promised his family he would visit his cousin, Ron, upon arriving in San Francisco—but the initial encounter was "a bit of a surprise".

"Ron's hair was a lot shorter than before and he had a funny look on his face, and a false smile that didn't suit him. He was cheerful, but something seemed to be missing that had been there before—I couldn't quite put my finger on what it was.

"Everyone else at the house seemed a bit weird and superficial too. There was this 'Hello...how are you!' routine, and everyone kept telling me 'Oh, you're Ron's cousin...he's such a great guy!' I must have heard that line a dozen times. Still, I hadn't seen Ron in three years, and we had once been pretty close...so it felt pretty good to be there."

Travel-weary, Benji soon found himself in the midst of the evening "lecture" and slide show, and he was baffled by the presentation and apparent scope of the "Creative Community Project". "It was corny...definitely not my kind of thing, but in other ways it seemed impressive—the businesses, the health clinics, the food give-aways, the doctors and lawyers that were supposedly involved. I couldn't figure it out at all."

When Ron said they were leaving for the "farm" that night, Benji didn't protest; he was in California to see Ron, and his cousin's description of Boonville made it sound like "a nice place to spend the weekend". They arrived at the camp well after two a.m. and went straight to bed.

"The next morning I woke up to someone playing the guitar and singing 'Red Red Robin'—and everyone jumping out of bed. I couldn't believe it...I mean it was eight a.m., I'd hardly slept and now this. I just rolled over to go back to sleep."

At his cousin's urging, however, Benji was soon up too—reluctantly taking part in the Boonville routine. Most of it seemed babyish and ridiculous, but he went along out of politeness, curiosity and a sense of obligation to his cousin, having little difficulty until the morning "sharing" session. Then, as members talked frankly of their "inner selves" and "gut feelings", Benji was left in an awkward position.

"I'm not in the habit of sharing my feelings with complete strangers," he recalls. "But at the same time, if I had just talked superficially, I would have felt rude, as though I was putting them down—so I was in a bit of a bind. My only real alternative was to get up and leave...but I had come all the way there to see Ron, and there was no way I was going to leave over something as petty as that."

So Benji opened up and talked a bit about his own life, his past and his thoughts on being a teacher. He didn't say a great deal, nonetheless he found that as he talked he began to feel somewhat "closer" to the group, and "sharing" became easier as the day progressed.

"Of course, not everyone would react like me," he acknowledges. "Some people might just have said 'screw it' and left—but at the time, it didn't seem like such a big thing to do."

The Boonville day unfolded almost identically to my own stay there: the same strange, frenzied activity; the singing, chanting and chooching; the thick starchy stews; and the dizzying intensity that left one without a moment for solitary thought. Like me, Benji soon found it unbearably claustrophobic.

"Holding hands all the time gave me the creeps, and the chanting really got on my nerves," he recalls. "The whole thing was just too 'groupy' for me—even though they were suggesting that it was my individualism that was really to blame. I just wasn't comfortable...I felt suffocated.

Each time Benji considered leaving, Ron would plead with him to stay just a bit longer, to give his project a chance; the same guilt-inducing tactic Benji himself would employ when Mike Kropveld came to visit months later.

So Benji stayed. The routine was "trying" but interesting, even "mysterious", for its very weirdness, and Benji had little reason to be suspicious. It was his cousin's project, and it seemed harmless enough: he had never heard of the Creative Community Project, let alone been aware that it was a front group for the Unification Church. As well, he was in the middle of nowhere with no way to return but his thumb, and Ron had promised him a tour of California when the "two day seminar" was over.

When he went to sleep that night, Benji was completely exhausted, falling into a "deep black sleep". Six hours later, he was up again and back into the Boonville routine; amazed to find that more than 100 members had arrived overnight, adding a powerful and moving enthusiasm to the camp's atmosphere. And as the second day rolled on, the Boonville environment began to have an unexpected effect.

Somehow, the bizarre, unrelenting activity and the intense personal dialogue began to create a mental vice that pushed Benji back into his own mind; as the day wore on and the talk became even more intimate, he began to feel increasingly uneasy. The whole experience was causing him to become extremely introspective, evoking depressing thoughts and questions, dredging up parts of him that he had almost forgotten existed in the busy pace of recent years.

In the previous few years, his life had changed, taken direction, moving on as if by its own force as he had "grown up"; now, suddenly, it was as if he had come to a way station, as if he could see his whole life stretched out before him on a dark, vast plain.

Men and women left suddenly unemployed after years of steady work often find themselves in crisis, confronting their sense of identity for the first time in their lives. Those who lose parents or mates often plunge into similar painful self-analysis, questioning things they have ignored or repressed throughout their lives. Others live with such "life crises" constantly, swallowing a steady dose of liquor or pills to keep these doubts and anxieties at the back of their minds.

Boonville provoked such a crisis in Benji, bringing him to explore the "back of his mind"; pushing him for the first time in a long while to ask himself who he was, what he was doing, and where he was going. He was not entirely satisfied with the answers.

"Before Boonville, I had thought I was at a point in my life where I knew what I was doing, as opposed to a few years earlier when I was still trying to figure things out. Sure, life wasn't a bed of roses—I had made certain compromises over recent years—but I figured I could live comfortably with them. I had a solid base to do what I wanted in life...friends, family...a profession I thought I wanted...

"But all that seemed to fall apart at Boonville. After just two days there my perspective was changing and I was starting to ask myself where was it all really going to take me. I hadn't really thought like that in years—I mean really analyzed where I was going and what the ramifications were. I had just decided to move ahead with my life and career, and stopped thinking about it...tucked my reservations into the back of my head.

"It was as if Boonville took me backwards...brought out the adolescent still inside me, the part of me that was still looking for something more, but had been covered up by time."

Benji remembered his youthful idealism, his belief that real change could be accomplished—and his desire to be part of that change somehow. He saw how he had grown more cynical with time, had compromised his idealism in gradual stages, rationalizing each stage by saying it was "practical". And as he realized this, old questions rose to the surface again.

"I found myself asking: 'why do I really want to teach?' Bethie especially would ask me that...The first night we had a long converstaion, and she talked a lot about her own experience as a teacher a few years earlier, which was very similar to my own. She brought out a lot of my own frustrations."

Benji talked about his two years working with emotionally disturbed kids, a frustrating time that saw him 'fixing kids up, then shipping them back to screwed-up homes...' "I mean you've got the kid for six hours a day...but all you're doing is fighting what's happening in the other eighteen."

He remembered several of the kids in his class—Eddy, for instance, a jumpy 13-year-old who Benji had finally got to "sit down long enough to start reading and learning...he even made a belt that he was really proud of...it was kind of exciting to watch him start to mature."

But every Monday morning, Eddy would show up at school as nervous and as at loose ends as ever, so finally Benji had gone to see the parents—only to find the same scene as always: an abandoned mother, alcoholic and living with a new boyfriend, while five kids shared the adjacent room.

"This is what the kid had to go home to...its what *all* these kids had to go home to...that's why they were so screwed up. It's so hard to even make a dent...so slow and frustrating...you can work for years thinking you're doing something, then suddenly find you haven't accomplished anything at all.

"Every time I work with kids, these kinds of problems are there. The only way to keep working is to believe that the few good things you achieve outweigh the thousand bad ones—which is how I usually see things—but not then in Boonville. Things were happening too fast. I was off balance because of the environment and couldn't think straight. And Bethie got there before me, as though she were reading my mind..."

"Sure there are some good things in teaching, Benji...a few nice moments," she said, "That's what makes it worth it...but in the end, where is it really going? What effect is it really going to have?...Isn't there more?..."

"And all that touched a part of me...these questions and doubts were inside me, but I had put a lid on them to give teaching a chance. They were things I already knew, but somehow she got them out again and heated them up...made me feel that all my arguments were just rationalizations to hide from the truth.

"Thinking back, it's easy to think of points to respond with; easy to slough off everything she said as hogwash and idealism; but back there, in that environment, it was all very real and hard to dispute. I was tired and overwhelmed, and there was this whole part of me that felt it couldn't disagree with what she was saying. Everything was true."

Bethie was not the only woman drawing the Boonville net tighter around Benji. There was also Linette, a lithe, enticing former dancer who had only recently come to Boonville herself. Benji was immediately attracted to her: he can still recall her dancing on a grassy hill one early morning, a perfect blue sky behind her, her hair and skirt swirling gently in the wind.

And there was Susan, a poised but ingenuous two-year member who accompanied Benji everywhere, drawing him into intimate discussions about their lives and past love affairs. "I don't usually talk about these things with many people. I'm reserved about my feelings, but in Boonville it's normal to talk about personal things after just a few minutes. In fact, it's *abnormal* and uptight not to. There's a certain amount of honesty, and that creates a bond. It made Susan and the others feel very close."

Benji's attraction to the women was initially sexual, but soon shifted to platonic friendship as he became tacitly aware of the Boonville attitude toward male-female relations: sex was something that came far later, and with much more meaning, not something to be doled out to a casual visitor like him.

"There was no tension or friction between sexes at Boonville. Normally, I'm not really even aware of sexual tension—I guess I've just accepted it as part of life and forgotten it. But at Boonville, in its absence, I became much more aware of how important it really is in the 'outside world'.

"There's always a certain amount of sexual jockeying, an uncertainty, because you never know exactly what the relationship is. I've always been a real perfectionist about women...I'm very choosy. If I start having a good time with someone, after a while, I always start finding faults and an excuse to leave. I do a lot of evaluating about how I want this person to fit into my life...and if I want her to at all. I get claustrophobic. I don't want to make a commitment...or put myself on the line.

"Susan and I talked a lot about sexual relationships—about the tension implicit in most male-female relationships. And at the same time as we were talking about all this, here was Susan sort of showing me the other side of the coin—a brother-sister kind of relationship...

"She was close, but she was no threat, because there was no possibility of an ordinary lovers' relationship. The brother-sister thing neutralized the relationship, made it safe. There was never a threat of a sexual relationship, so there was no need for me to evaluate it, and that allowed me to get closer to her...I'd only been there a couple of days, but already I was starting to feel as close to these women as I did to people I'd known for years.

"And the closer I got, the more I felt that they were just like me; and the harder it got to maintain my idea that they were nice kids, but screwed up and into something weird ...while *I* was *normal*."

That night, an older "family" member named Stoller gave a long, and moving account of his life—and the parallels to his own life unnerved Benji. Like him, Stoller was Jewish, with one set of grandparents from Poland and the other from Russia. Stoller told the group that his own parents were a break in the family history: settlers in North America, seeking material success to found a family in the New World.

But Stoller said that he could not identify with this; instead he felt more attached to the older, simple values of his grandfather's generation—an idea that struck a chord deep in Benji. Soon, Stoller's remarks were flushing up countless old memories from Benji's mind—memories of his childhood days and his long-forgotten relationship with his own grandfather.

"I was crazy about my grandfather. He took me everywhere—anywhere I wanted to go—walks to the park, the movies, and on Saturday mornings to the synagogue, where he was very respected and everyone would come and ask his advice."

Listening to Stoller, Benji recalled childhood scenes with his grandfather with intense clarity: taking a walk down a back alley together, shopping on the Main, sitting on his grandfather's lap in a small park. He remembered being six years old and standing in the huge synagogue, awed by the powerful music and hugging his grandfather's pleated trouser leg as the old man stroked his chin and conversed in smiling, solemn tones to men in yamulkas gathered around him for a piece of wisdom.

Later Benji would watch his *zaidye* make wine in the basement, fermenting it like an old chemist. There was something simple, slow, magical about his grandfather; and the long-buried memories of the experience swept over Benji like waves that night in Boonville, provoking a near-religious experience.

"I think that was really the beginning of my sense of religious feeling. Before that I'd always been very critical of religion, considering it as too superstitious, but at Boonville, I began to identify religion with my grandfather, even though I still had no idea that the group had a religious base.

"My grandfather represented so much of the spiritual 'ideal' that everyone at Boonville kept saying was part of us; the part our parents had rejected for the good life, the American way. He was the glue of the family. When he died our family was never quite the same. There was more petty bickering...fewer family ties. No one would take the services at Passover seriously any more...they'd be 10 minutes in between periods of the hockey games so nobody would miss the play-offs—including me.

"So by getting me to associate religion with my grandfather, it suddenly became a warm thing that held the family together—not as I had always seen it before, a crutch filled with hypocrisy. They never even had to bring religion up; they brought it out of me instead."

By the conclusion of Stoller's talk, Benji was extremely moved. He felt that Stoller was talking to him; about his life, his family, his inner doubts. He felt as though he had been put in touch with a part of himself that was buried under years of twentieth century life, "a sense of simplicity and wonder that Boonville had somehow brought out of me.

"I saw my grandfather. He had no TV, no car; he lived in his district, saw his friends and made his wine. He was a simple man...Then I saw my father and his generation—caught between their human selves and their need to survive and get ahead in the modern world. My father was tied up in consumer society. He needed his car, his TV, and his house, and in order to afford them he had to take part in the rat race, get involved in business deals that exploited the third world and compromised his humanity. And all that kept him from becoming really happy.

"I could see his good sides too; a goodness, a warmth toward people and an honesty that I loved him for. Yet at the same time, I could see where he was a victim of his era. He and his friends were caught up in another reality—a more materialistic one that didn't appeal to me. My reality, my ambition, were more in line with my grandfather; slow, wise, solid, earthy. I started to realize that as a child he had been a God to me; and in Boonville's environment, he seemed almost God-like again."

When he went to sleep that night, Benji felt a tremendous uncertainty, pierced by instances of dread, "as though I were seeing things clearly for the first time in years, and there were gray clouds around even the good things in my life...

"I felt unsure about a lot of things in my life, but at the same time I felt a sense of new possibilities. An idealism I'd buried years ago seemed alive again, and with it a fear that if I went back to my old life again, without doing anything about it, I would lose this vision and sink into my old routine again. I would miss a once-in-a-lifetime opportunity.

"But the problem was that I wasn't really examining things and testing them against me and my own ideas. There was no time or space to think in Boonville, so everything just seemed to sink in like truths. I had no perspective. Everything they were saying seemed terribly true, and I couldn't find the energy to dispute it.

"Still, it wasn't just the environment of Boonville that got me. That's too easy an out. They were also reaching some part of me; getting me to go along with them."

By the middle of the next day in Boonville, Benji was in trouble. The camp's unrelenting claustrophobia and his growing self-doubts had closed in like a stranglehold, creating a terrifying psychological threat.

"My whole life seemed in crisis. Who was I? Where would

I go next? What could I do to change my life? Everything seemed all muddled up.

"I knew I agreed with lots of things in Boonville—the community, the togetherness, the honesty and idealism—and I was starting to feel a growing guilt about leaving it behind. But I also knew I needed perspective badly; my thinking was very, very confused."

The psychological pressure was so intense that suddenly, it had physical effects.

"My head felt like it was splitting open from pressure, as though something inside me were swollen and about to burst. My body felt light...I was dizzy and scared. My head was stuffed with conflicting ideas and emotions; thoughts were racing through my mind then stopping short. My mood was changing wildly from happy to miserable."

As he became aware of the tremendous impact Boonville was suddenly having on him, Benji became frightened at his changes; frightened he might actually crack-up—something he had never considered remotely possible before. Panic set in.

"There was a sense of incredible flight. My adrenalin began pumping like I was being chased for my life. I was overflowing with emotion and self-doubts. Anger, tension, confusion, fear...I felt I had to get out of there fast. A voice inside me was saying, 'You've got to get out of here, Benji, you've got to get out!'"

He confided his dilemma to Susan, told her he was coming apart at the seams and had to leave Boonville quickly to get some perspective on the project and himself; but she turned the statement on its head to induce more guilt at his desire to leave. She told him it was like "meeting someone, falling wildly in love with them and then announcing after three days, that you want to go away for a couple of weeks to think about whether you're really in love..."

"That really made an impression on me at the time. It made me feel even more guilty about wanting to leave Boonville," remembers Benji. "The way she put it, it seemed to be part of my pattern of non-commitment, as though I were looking for another excuse to leave something or someone behind,...searching for a flaw so I could avoid committing myself again."

As he walked away from her, Benji tried to overcome his sense of guilt and fear, and concentrate on leaving; he conjured up a mental picture of himself packing his bag and hitching down the road. He feared a nervous breakdown if he stayed any longer, as though his mind would actually "come apart". No matter what Susan said, he had to get out of Boonville.

His only barrier was his cousin Ron and the need to explain his sudden departure. As Benji approached him, he made a last desperate effort to pull himself together, steeling himself for a possible confrontation. But his cousin hardly reacted at all, ignoring Benji's obvious distress "as though nothing out of the ordinary was happening". Casually, he suggested that Benji catch the "last lecture", since a van would soon be heading back to San Francisco, anyway. Then he threw his arm gently around Benji's shoulder and started walking him back toward the lecture hall.

For an instant Benji hesitated, poised to break loose and flee in panic. Then he caught himself and fought down his inner terror and the desperate urge to run. "I had a sense that I was the one who was acting crazy, making a big deal out of this one last lecture, when I could get a lift back once it was over.

"Everything there looked so innocuous...just a bunch of people up in the country listening to some weird lectures and trying to get to know each other. What was I getting so paranoid about? I had to get hold of myself, start acting rationally. I'd catch the van in a couple of hours..."

So Benji ended up going back "like a lamb" to the "final" lecture, where all the energy, frustration and strength he had built up seemed suddenly to dissipate—as though whatever had been building up inside him had imploded, rather than exploded, "I don't know exactly what happened, but it was a really key point. Something changed drastically, as though a very powerful force were gripping me...as though I'd been wrestling for my life and suddenly got very, very tired, pinned to the mat by the sheer weight of my opponent. Nothing I could do would budge him. I lost my resistance. The intensity of my desire to go just seemed to surrender, and it never returned."

Soon after, a van heading back to San Francisco loaded up with a few family members, but Benji was not on it. Instead, like several other recruits who had come up with him, Benji stood silently transfixed, "as though I were watching a film". As the van disappeared in the distance and he realized he was staying, a huge weight seemed to come off his shoulders and his body was gripped with a "strange, disattached feeling. My mouth was parched and numb; there was a tremendous tension in my body, a nervous anxiety that sizzled inside me."

Electricity seemed to be pulsing, rushing through his veins in a raw buzzing sensation that would last all evening. And the same current of electricity seemed to engulf everyone who had stayed: Bethie, Susan, Ron and the other recruits, as though all of them were linked to a single source of power. His body felt lighter, as though striving to break free of him and float alone through space.

"I had brought out all my problems, and now I felt as though I had thrown them away...They weren't my problems anymore."

That night, sleeping on the cold, hard floor of the "Chicken Palace", Benji awoke and saw a brilliant white light as far as he could discern—so bright that "if I had opened my eyes, it would have blinded me". He shielded his eyes and the light enveloped him, "warming and soothing me, draining the tension from my body". He felt as though someone or something was blowing a large breath of air into his lungs, then he slowly exhaled and fell into a perfect, tranquil sleep.

When he awoke in the morning, he could not be sure whether the strange experience had been a dream, a vision or reality, but it seemed terribly important to him. He had never before believed in revelations, but it seemed as though he had been sent a signal, "telling me I was through the impasse, and my decision to stay longer at Boonville had been right".

He felt better than he had in days: his questions and doubts seemed to have faded, his fear and anxiety were gone. The world looked strangely different, closer, as though he were a living part of "something bigger".

Something in him or the world around him had shifted, and though he didn't know what it was, one thing was devastatingly clear: there was no going back.

Benji's experience may seem somewhat dramatic to this point, but it is borne out by the accounts of many ex-Moonies. Testimonies usually describe a period during which formerly "stable" individuals suddenly feared themselves near emotional collapse from an assault of introspective questions and growing self-doubt.

The emotional crisis often culminates in powerful physical sensations: one woman spoke of "lighting up like a pinball machine"; another felt like the blood in her veins was "on fire". Finally there is a breaking point at which people find their personalities "coming apart"—not disintegrating into chaos or madness, but settling into a larger "something".

Typical was the experience of our friend Mike Kropveld, who initially went to Boonville to visit Benji, but soon fell under the camp's spell.

Mike, like Benji, was at first skeptical of the Boonville routine; he stayed only because his best friend, Benji, kept promising him they'd be leaving soon for a "trip down the coast". Like Benji, he had never so much as heard of the Moonies or their alleged brainwashing techniques; he went along with the Boonville routine out of a combination of politeness and mild guilt at not wanting to "put them down". He asked so many questions the first day, that he was jokingly nicknamed "Mr. Negativity".

But after two days of Boonville's onslaught, Mike too felt his defenses drifting away, as he retreated inside his own mind.

"The whole thing is very introspective. You look back at your whole life...what you're doing, where you're going... and let's be honest, what are most people really doing that's so fulfilling they can't imagine better? Most people are moving slowly, compromising in a lot of areas so they can get by.

"Me, I thought a lot about how my social commitment had faded. When I was younger, social issues were my bread and butter, but after a few years, I started to realize just where I stood in relation to the system; how futile it was for an individual to try to do anything. I realized I wasn't going to change the world by marching. Things were too complicated. So I kind of settled down. I ended up working with retarded kids, and living my own life.

"But in Boonville, with all those people believing they could change things, a lot of my old feelings started to come out again, and with them a sense of guilt at having given up too easily. A lot of the things they were saying seemed true. Maybe I was living a selfish life in some ways. Maybe I should start thinking more about others...just my daily lunch could probably keep someone in the Third World alive for days.

"Selfishness sort of gets redefined there. Its not something you're doing; it's what you're *not* doing."

Mike too was besieged by women—the ubiquitous Bethie, and a girl from Montreal who drew him into deep personal conversations. He talked about his work, his feelings for his family, and his friends back home.

"Two pretty solid couples I knew had just broken up after years together, and that had sort of depressed me. I started thinking that maybe you had to be more prepared for a relationship. I always knew relationships needed work, but at Boonville I started thinking that maybe the work was needed before a relationship could even begin. Maybe a lot of people weren't in close enough touch with themselves to be in a relationship...maybe we should be looking after ourselves first."

By the third day, Mike's needs had begun to shift from wild optimism to stark depression. He felt like "an emotional tennis ball. It was a very intense time. What am I doing? What are my relationships like? Where is my life going? Can I still change it? I could deal with a lot of the questions they were raising, a little at a time, but they had me in a giant psychotherapy session, confronting my whole life at a single moment. It was a huge rush of ideas, with no time or space to absorb them.

"It's like a funnel on top of a bottle. If you pour stuff in slowly, everything goes; but take the funnel away and it floods."

Then, like Benji, the psychological pressure brought on physical sensations. "My head felt like it was physically expanding, so full of thoughts and ideas...connections, conflicts, relationships; coming to terms with every aspect of my life at a single moment. And all this in an alien atmosphere without a second of relief. It was too much for me to handle; I thought my head would blow up."

When Mike went to sleep, he was dizzy and disturbed. His head felt "as though it was inflated three inches", and he fell into a troubled sleep. When he awoke the next morning, "everything had changed". His head had stopped swelling, his anxiety and inner doubts were gone. For the first time, he realized that he saw things with a "new clarity, as though a jigsaw puzzle had been thrown in the air, then fallen to the ground in a perfect pattern.

"I still didn't know exactly what that pattern meant, but I knew it had something to do with Boonville. I was ready to stay there until I found out what."

Mike and Benji's "conversion" experiences are similar to those reported by many former members of the Unification Church and other cults. Flo Conway and Jim Siegelman interviewed members of numerous present day cults for their book *Snapping;* they found that most had shared a "snapping" moment similar to Mike and Benji's when their personalities "came apart" in a rush of sensations.

For example, a young member of the Divine Light Mission told them that he was "initiated" in a pitch black room at three am, after little sleep, by someone who "came swishing out of the darkness. I felt his fingers on my eyes and I saw a light that seemed to stab down from the outer darkness. It came from somewhere behind me and created a figure eight of pure white light. It lasted for a brief period of time, and I was blown away by it."

In *Varieties of Religious Experience,* William James recorded similar conversion experiences in earlier times. For instance, 18th century evangelist John Wesley could bring mobs of people to their knees, many of whom "leaped like frogs and exhibited every grotesque and hideous contortion of the face and limbs...getting down on all fours growling, snapping the teeth, and barking like dogs."

After such experiences, people often reported a state of clarity much like that of Mike and Benji. One 19th century convert testified:

"In an instant the bandage had fallen from my eyes; and not one bandage only, but the whole manifold of bandages in which I had been brought up. One after another they rapidly disappeared, even as the mud and ice disappears under the rays of the burning sun."

Most North Americans can accept such historical conversions as a product of supersitition and lack of education, but we are alarmed at the ability of present-day cults to entrap modern, educated young people.

Harvard psychiatrist John Clark conducted in-depth interviews with more than 100 former cult members, many from the Unification Church. Dr. Clark found that at least 60 per cent of them were "bright, normal developing young people" who were lured in by the groups' powerful techniques. American sociologists David G. Bromley and Anson D. Shupe studied the Unification Church for three years and came to similar conclusions. Those interviewed appeared "to have been no more depressed or tension-ridden than most other young people."

My own research into the Unification Church confirms these findings and suggests a further detail: most of the brighter and more articulate members I met (such as Benji, Mike and Bethie), fell into the cult while visiting former friends at Boonville. Many ex-Moonies also break Church members into two categories: the "seekers", picked up easily by street proselytizing, and the "normal ones", lured to Boonville by former friends and lovers.

These people do not come to Boonville troubled and searching for meaning in their lives; they come simply to see what their friends are doing—whereupon Boonville's assault rips apart their complacency and finds the "seeker" inside them. For some, the vulnerable spot is a lack of fulfillment in their work or personal lives; for others, the guilt of being modern "consumers" who have compromised their past ideals. Their own unused potential is used as a weapon to push them into extreme introspection...and further.

As Dr. Clark concludes in his paper "Manipulation of Madness": "They (cults) are embarking upon a draconian experiment...one which no ethical scientist would consider taking...a healthy person with a basic neurosis was having it transformed into an acute obsession...*psychosis was being imposed.*"

Then, poised at the abyss of nervous collapse, the recruit is offered only one avenue of escape, which he takes in sheer desperation: he fastens onto the group to escape his pain. It is not said, but it is implicit: as long as he remains in Boonville and continues his inner exploration, he will be accepted, loved—even respected, for the courage to face his problems and try to change.

The recruit did not need such support when he arrived at Boonville, but now, with his sense of identity collapsing, he needs it desperately; he clings to the group like a raft in a storm, carried along on a wave with no idea of where it will break, knowing only that for the time being it will keep him sane and alive.

It is a release to what psychiatrist Joost Meerloo called "the inner traitor in all of us", in his classic 1950's text on brainwashing, *The Rape of the Mind*. "Men yield primarily because at some point they are overwhelmed by their unconscious conflicts," says Dr. Meerloo. "These conflicts, kept under control in normal circumstances, come to the surface under the strain of menticidal pressure (brainwashing).

"It is as if the future mental patient preferred to surrender to an outward enemy, rather than to the inward enemies of disease and nervous breakdown." (My italics.)

This conversion process is a giant leap-frogging from one reality to another. It virtually peels the recruit's identity from his body, and jars him loose from his ordinary way of perceiving the world. According to Dr. Margaret Thaler Singer, a San Francisco psychiatrist who interviewed hundreds of present and former cult members, it often results in the glassy-eyed stare and religious visions that marked Benji's experience. Other changes may include impotence, arrested growth of facial hair and the voice becoming high and shrill.

Yet for all their power, these changes do not signify the "creation" of a Moonie. The resulting loss of self may be sufficient to create a new charismatic, or a Billy Graham convert, but it is not enough to send the recruit out flower-selling and proselytizing for Moon; in fact, he usually does not yet even know that Moon exists.

If the recruit were to return to the world and his old "connections" at this point, says Dr. Clark, he would likely fall back into his old life, with little remaining but a sense of wonder at a remarkable experience (and a possible willingness to make regular contributions to the group that "saved" him.) But just as evangelist John Wesley discovered 100 years earlier that he required regular "study groups" if his members were not to "slide back into misery", Moon too requires continuing—though far greater supervision of the "convert".

The new recruit is weak and frightened; he has lost his sense of identity and is desperately in need of something to restore or replace it, but he is not a "Moonie". He is only the raw material with which the making of a Moonie will begin.

11

"The next three weeks were a fog," says Benji of the period immediately following his "conversion" and he remembers few details. Boonville's frantic routine seemed to catapult on, as Benji clung desperately to it, burying his newly discovered self-doubt in the group's frenzied activity.

"Every day was just a carbon copy of the previous one ...incredibly busy," he says. "But as I kept going through the same motions and the same lectures every day, time started to lose all sense. My memory and thinking got duller and duller..."

Dr. John Clark refers to this post-conversion period as "conversion maintenance", and it is an appropriate term. It is a holding pattern: a time to consolidate the break with the recruit's old identity; to distance his memories of family, friends, school, work and reality; to heighten his increasingly desperate dependence on the group. By the time the maintenance period is over, says Dr. Clark, "safety and sanity are deemed possible only within the cult."

Most ex-members describe this early period as a sort of nether world in which they ghost-walked, dumbfounded; uncertain of where they were heading but terrified of returning to their former lives by the emotional wounds now associated with them. This was the period during which Mike Kropveld left Boonville, and the experience had already severely crippled him.

"I was a very vulnerable, frightened person," Mike recalls

of the time following his conversion. "If I was off by myself for just a few minutes, a feeling of loneliness seemed to cut right through me...then as soon as I'd be back with the group again, there'd be a terrific sense of relief...a sense of closeness and growing euphoria."

In exchange for this now-vital support of the group, the recruit is required to "share" more and more details of his inner self during daily confession periods, excavating his mind for further details of his sordid, selfish life. Some recruits are encouraged to talk about their family problems, others about their greedy consumerism, and as one female ex-Moonie publicly testified, many were grilled for hours on the explicit details of their sex lives: "every boy or girl I had made love to, the times I had masturbated, the time I seduced my younger brother..."

Benji was encouraged to talk of his past relationships with women and work; focusing on the egocentricism and lack of commitment he was now convinced they demonstrated. The more he exaggerated negative aspects of his life, the more enthusiastically he was received. Day by day, his stories grew grimmer and more incriminating, as "I started to believe what I was saying and experience a growing sense of relief at the life I had escaped.

"The more I talked about my life, the more I felt separated from it, until eventually...my old life seemed almost never to have existed."

All this is well mapped out by the Church's leaders. Former Unification Church instructor Gary Scharff says he was told to use the first three days to locate and "hook" the recruit's weaknesses, the following seven days to "reel them in", and the next 21 to have them go through old experiences and "re-digest their lives".

"Give them an experience of re-birth," was a recruiting instruction Scharff copied into his notebook at the time. "They must reckon with the past and get a new start...then they can become a part of the body of the Messiah."

As the maintenance period proceeds, says Dr. Clark, the

past "seems almost never to have existed" and the recruit comes more and more to exist in the now. "Reality becomes the present and includes in it elements of supernatural, terrifying magical thought..."

Benji concurs. "Towards the end of the fourth week at Boonville, the idea of God seemed very real to me, very close by. The less validity my own life had, the more I sensed that I belonged to something bigger. There were incredibly 'full' moments. For the first time in my life, I was beginning to think that there was something called the Truth, and that Boonville was somehow tied up with it. I was grappling to understand it.

"My old world seemed to have become dark and black and evil, while Boonville was becoming a bright, shining hope. I still didn't know where it was I was heading...but at last I had the feeling that I was coming out of the fog. I could almost make out what was ahead, and as I could, I wanted to see it even more and more clearly."

Benji was ready to make a commitment. His old life was obsolete, utterly without value, his only hope lay in the future, with the Creative Community Project. The "holding pattern" was over. It had been only a month since Benji had arrived for a quick visit with his cousin, but already he was ready to leave Boonville and follow the group—wherever it led.

In leaving Boonville, the recruit takes the next major step toward becoming a Moonie: committing himself to full-time membership in the Creative Community Project. Some are not "ready" to make this commitment for as long as three months, but most are prepared by the end of the first month.

Shupe and Bromley, studying a Unification Church recruiting camp in Texas, found that only 15 per cent of the recruits had actually made a full-time commitment to the organization after the first three days, but a full 60 percent had made it after the first month. Benji joined on his 25th day, actually signing a contractual agreement pledging to remain a member for at least three months. Soon after, he agreed to turn over $2000 in savings, as a gesture of "faith".

Other ex-Moonies say they were required to make similar overt commitments. Ex-Moonie Jan Kaplan told me that she ripped the pages out of her diary at this point, symbolizing that her life was starting anew; others underwent three-day fasts; most agreed to throw out their clothes and accept communal possessions and a short haircut. Some recruits change their names, the men taking solemn biblical ones such as Noah and Jeremiah, the women more breezy ones like Muffy and Poppy.

The changes are telling symbols, for this is perhaps the crucial step in becoming a Moonie. It is here that some of the most profound implications of cult behaviour can be found; yet here that most cult-watchers lose sight of the winding psychological trail.

To this point, the recruit has been a creature of his emotions, a shredded personality taken to the brink of psychosis, then "saved", clinging to the group for protection from his still raw inner wounds. Now the nature of the commitment to the group alters drastically: it shifts from an emotional attachment to a powerful intellectual commitment.

"Feelings are what have gotten man into trouble throughout history," echoes the very first Boonville lecture. Now, after four weeks of travelling through the Boonville "fog", the implications are at last clear.

"We must *overcome* our feelings...change them and bring them into line with our new ideals. We must have the strength and discipline to build ourselves into *restored personalities*...so that each of us can become a better person. *God can cure your disease...he can change your character.*"

In committing himself to stay, the recruit is not simply agreeing to join the group to serve God and build a "better world"; he is also pledging to try and build a "better self", to remake himself into a "good person". It is a tremendous task; in the words of the Church's own 120-day training manual, it means: "I must deny my way of thinking, my way of feeling, my way of talking, everything. My desire, my hope, my joy, my will must be placed on the altar and given to God... Nothing belongs to myself anymore...everything belongs to God. I have nothing."

So it was for Benji: "The commitment was terribly important, the most important thing I'd ever done. Up until then, I had just been hanging around Boonville out of a mixture of guilt, fear and idealism and I was often participating only half-heartedly. But now I was promising to stay with the group for three months and try to remake myself, even though I had no idea what that involved. I was convinced that I had lived a small, narrow existence...that all my values and ideas, "concepts" as we called them, had been brainwashed into me by the evil, selfish world I had lived in. Now I was agreeing to try and overcome those concepts, no matter how hard that was. If we were going to change the world, first we had to change man...and that meant changing *me*. Everything about me...

"The way I thought, the values and feelings I had, my attachment to my parents, even my need for sleep and food, all these were parts of the old me I was rejecting. I had to transcend them...get rid of those parts of me and build myself over again from scratch...though I had no idea where that would eventually take me..."

In principle, Benji's aims could sound almost noble and idealistic, but there was a hideous catch. Since the recruit was still just a "spiritual child", explains Gary Scharff, he was not yet capable of deciding what constituted a "good person". So all he could do in the meantime was adopt the group's standards; serve the "common good" rather than his own, follow an outside model.

"Good was defined as living for other people...evil was when you lived for yourself," sums up Scharff. "So to become a good person, you had to deny your own feelings and desires and devote yourself to the group...and that meant obeying without question anything that the leaders told you to do. Serving *whole purpose* rather than small purpose—God rather than self."

The recruit was agreeing to obey the group standards "in all situations—even when his own "selfish" conscience told him to do otherwise," explains Scharff. "That meant obeying Reverend Moon...because that's where the group's decisions were coming from, even if he didn't know it at the time."

San Francisco psychologist and professor of psychiatry Dr. Margaret Thaler Singer worked with the U.S. Army in Korea after World War II examining allegedly brainwashed prisoners of war. She has since interviewed more than 350 active and former members of North American cults. According to Dr. Singer, this moment of "commitment" is a critical step in the indoctrination process of the Unification Church: the point at which new recruits completely expose themselves to what she terms the "soul engineering" that lies ahead.

"In the early weeks, a lot of these kids are just wounded and frightened," says Dr. Singer. "They're staying with the group to ease the emotional hurt that they feel. But once they've agreed to treat their own thoughts and feelings as *dangerous inner enemies*...to trust the group before they trust themselves...they're starting to lose *all* touch with their old selves..."

From this point on, when the group tells the recruit to sacrifice food, he must readily go hungry; if it tells him to lie or steal, he must obey; if it tells him to believe something—anything—he must strive to do so, no matter how much it defies the bounds of his old concepts. His own doubts and hesitations are to be seen as his inner weaknesses; a product of his self-centred thinking.

He must supress them and do what must be done for God until such time as he is strong enough to understand, strong enough to have a wider vision that will take account of the whole picture. "Later I will understand...now I must be humble to God."

In short, the recruit has found a way to by-pass his own

feelings and moral values; yet to rationalize this moral surrender as an act of inner strength and discipline. The more his "old self" protests what he is doing, the stronger is his "new self" for its ability to ignore the inner cries and "stay on the right track".

The recruit's old identity is capped and almost completely buried. In the words of Dr. John Clark: "At this point consciousness is a very narrow piece of functioning...there is only the last little bit needed to completely seal off the memory of the old person...and chanting provides the tool."

In the days immediately before his departure from Boonville, the recruit has been repeatedly warned of the difficulties he will face on returning to the sinful world; a world so evil, so selfish that it will threaten his new faith and commitment, tempt his old "concepts" out of their hiding place in his mind.

He must be prepared to combat not just the evil outside, but the evil and selfishness it will provoke inside him. "It is so easy to backslide." To resist these attacks, he is taught to "centre"—to chant—a technique of "positive thinking" that will help him to concentrate (centre) on the group's teaching and fight off attacks of "spaced out" or "negative" thought. It will bring him back to God "like a lighthouse in a fog".

"You learn to use it to stop your mind from wandering or drifting into negative areas," recalls Benji. "You tell yourself over and over: don't wander...don't think...just do what you're supposed to be doing. Do it...DO IT! That way, if a negative thought comes into your head, you don't dwell on it or waste time trying to figure it out...you just run over it and do what you have to. DO IT!"

In their first days back in San Francisco, Benji and the other new recruits were kept in a special "halfway house" adapting to these new techniques so they could go out in the world alone. Within a week, the chant had become an effective means of combating the treacherous inner voice within Benji—the weak former self that he was forever trying to repress, but which haunted him nonetheless. No matter how great his resolve, he never knew when it might suddenly attack: a craving for food or sleep while he was busy raising money for God; a flash of some childhood memory lingering in his mind and slowing his work pace; perhaps even a doubt or challenge to the authority of the Project itself.

No sooner did the treacherous thought or desire materialize than the chant would be there to automatically stifle it—a sentry protecting the new found purity of his mind. Hunger, fatigue, lust, laziness, doubt, these were simply old "concepts" still dormant within him. They must be overcome.

"You must not sleep much, eat much, rest much. You must work day and night to make this great task a reality. You must move on right to the moment of death..." said the study guide. There was no limit to what Benji could do, if he overcame his negative concepts.

Already he was living on only one or two meagre meals a day, sleeping less than four hours a night—yet feeling stronger, closer to God all the time. The world could be changed if you gave "one-oh-oh"...one hundred per cent. "BRING IN THE MONEY...STAY AWAKE!...SMASH OUT DOUBTS!" he would chant whenever he felt weakness coming on, and soon, the weakness would fade and disappear.

According to Gary Scharff, the chant was the key to establishing "total control" over the recruit. "Up until then, you were prepared to obey, but you always had to have an older brother or sister around to tell you what to do.

"But we wanted more...we wanted the source for that authority to be *within you*. A real Moonie is the cult's own agent in indoctrinating himself...and the chant was how that was established."

Originally the chant was used only to psyche Benji up when he felt negative thoughts threatening him; but as the days passed, Benji, like most of his brothers and sisters took to chanting to himself any time he was unoccupied. It became a means of keeping his mind filled during idle moments, preempting any possibility of "evil" thoughts invading by keeping his mind filled with "positive" ones.

Idle seconds were dangerous terrain, a possible foothold for the selfishness still lurking in his heart. So instead, Benji silently chanted. He chanted as he walked through the streets; he chanted as he rode the bus to the University to look for members; he even kept a light chant going during idle seconds of conversation with potential recruits he met on the street. While they responded to his approach, Benji would be secretly chanting "Bring in the money...BRING IN THE MONEY!"—psyching up, psyching up as they spoke their selfish prattle, so that he could once again give them God's word.

"Glory to Heaven. Peace on Earth. BRING IN THE MONEY!"

Eventually, within only weeks of his return to the city, Benji would be actively participating in massive, daily group chants of such intensity they would provoke near-mystical experiences among members. He would also spend hours in feverish prayer, similarly intended to eradicate all glimmers of critical thought or doubt.

"Oh Heavenly Father...Please, please, please forgive me for not giving my one-oh-oh selling flowers today. Oh, I've been so unrighteous and so selfish, please, please, please forgive me Father!"

At least three hours a day would be spent in such intensive prayer and chant to psyche members up for their contact with the evil, outside world. The resulting scenes would be reminiscent of the orgiastic "two minute hate" in George Orwell's *1984*, with members repeating the same chant over and over for half an hour, until many were writhing on the ground in "ecstasy", pounding their fists in the air and shrieking at the top of their lungs:

"GLORY TO HEAVEN! PEACE ON EARTH! BLESS HEAVENLY FATHER!"

"The first few minutes of it were always the hardest," recalls Benji. "You'd just be doing it by rote, fighting it out till you'd feel it. But then you'd sort of warm into it...get into the familiar rhythm again, where you start working on a higher and higher pitch...until all thoughts, all worries, all doubts are dissolved into a great *gush* of feeling; as though you were being carried away on a giant wave, totally enveloped."

After half an hour of chanting, members would link hands and experience a "sense of remarkable calm", then a slow, rising strength and a fierce togetherness and determination, "as though we were one giant, merging creature—with one mind, one purpose—ready to do anything...*anything.*"

With this tool, the work of destroying the recruit's personality is now complete. Private thoughts no longer exist; chanting has replaced thinking, and offered as its reward the increasing frequency of ecstasy.

Not only has the "old self" been imprisoned in a subterranean chamber of the mind, but any possibility of escape has been eliminated by plastering over the cracks in the cell wall with the sealant of the chant. Thought and feeling are now the enemy: no sooner do they begin to operate than they trigger the chant like a burglar alarm, to seal off the prisoner's cage again. In effect, the recruit is his own jailer.

Whatever thoughts, feelings, relationships, ideas or passions had made up the individual have now been neutralized; they will no longer play a role in determining his future. In the words of Gary Scharff: "The line between self and other is now eroded. Good feeling comes from accepting all the cult's tenets as your own, as coming from within you...there is no longer an inner voice that talks to you."

Ted Patrick, a notorious one-man crusade who has deprogrammed more than 1500 cult members sees the chant as a kind of self-hypnosis "that comes in a million forms and every cult uses...it can be induced by repeating a chant, a word, a group of words, by meditation, yoga, tapes, records, the Bible, the cult's books, any card in the deck."

"First they empty your brain. Then they stuff it with their

ideas, and then they seal you in the new world forever with the chanting technique."

Dr. Margaret Singer agrees. "The chant prevents the member from ever, ever connecting up with his old self again. There is no conscience, no reason...no rational thought going on. Self is totally obliterated. Now they can start running the program like a tape...and the kids have no defense against it."

"Programming" is the last, and in many ways the easiest stage in the making of a Moonie. Once the old self has been cancelled, the recruit can be gradually molded into his new identity; virtually anything the Church tells him must be rationalized and absorbed. Those who still show signs of resistance are quickly sent back to Boonville for further training.

The recruit's hair has already been shorn and his clothes "communalized"; now he is introduced to the rigors of a "life for God" in the Creative Community Project. This, he soon discovers, involves three central activities: recruiting, fund-raising and chanting. Within days of returning to San Francisco and making the three-month commitment, Benji was voluntarily rising at 4.45 a.m. to chant and study the Divine Principle. At 5:30 "late wakers" would arise for several more hours of feverish group praying, chanting and singing. Silence was observed until 7:15 a.m. and a liquid fast until noon.

At 10:30, members were sent to work at recruiting new members, selling flowers in the street or working in one of the Project's many businesses. Benji usually did recruiting or flower-selling, and he often went without any solid food until suppertime. At 6 p.m., he would return to Washington House to meet whatever new recruits had been rounded up during the day. I'd be starving by then and would stuff myself with the daily casserole," he recalls, though fish, meat or other protein substitutes were never served. "An egg in the soup was a real treat."

At 10:30 p.m., when the nightly lecture and slide show had ended and recruits had either left or gone up to Boonville, Benji and the other members would spend several hours cleaning up tons of dirt and dishes from 75 people eating dinner. As mopping and cleaning continued, exhaustion would overcome him and his mind would become foggy. "I'd start falling asleep on my feet and have to chant to keep awake."

Sometime between 12:30 and 2:30 a.m., he would retire to the crowded room he "shared" with about 10 other people. There was no T.V., no radio, no newspapers or other reading material. He would not need them, crashing into a dreamless black sleep for an average of four hours.

In later weeks, he would often be awakened in the dead of night to participate in a special "family" chant that the San Francisco area Church maintained in serial fashion, 24 hours a day. Every second night he would be hauled from bed at 3 a.m. to splash water on his face, hurry into a white shirt and tie and rush downstairs to relieve the previous "chanter". He would chant till 3:30 a.m., then hurry back to sleep on the hard wood floor until his 4:45 wake-up hour.

One day a week, most members would do a water-only fast and three-day fasts were regularly encouraged. Sundays provided the only real "break" in the routine. At 4 a.m. often without having slept, members would board Project buses, and drive to a "holy spot" at a nearby mountain for prayer and chanting. The drive back to the city in the early morning light would see many people falling asleep in their seats, only to be woken by a nudge from a mindful neighbor convinced that "the more sleep we sacrificed...the stronger we would eventually become".

"Sometimes I feel so sick, intolerably," said the study guide. "But I don't worry about that so much. I think that even if I am exhausted and die it is natural. So do your best. When you exhaust your energy and accomplish the goal you will become a perfect object for God and you will be revived. This is the Principle."

Within this maelstorm of unrelenting activity, meagre food and little sleep, the remaining traces of Benji's personality were gradually replaced by the Moonie prototype. Dress, manner and speech were all pushed to become more "God-centred": Gary Scharff's notebook contains instructions specifying the desirable posture, gaze and even eyelash angle for the "perfect soldier of God".

Speech was transformed too, as the language was loaded with what Yale psychiatrist Robert Jay Lifton has termed "thought-terminating cliches". Conscience and values were reduced to disposable "concepts"; the word "sincere" was inverted in sense, to mean being true to God (the group) rather than oneself; and "love" was a universal term to justify anything one did for God, regardless of how unscrupulous. In this fashion, acts such as lying, cheating and stealing could be dismissed as "heavenly deception".

Like the Ministry of Truth in *1984* which declares "Peace is War and War is Peace! Democracy is tyranny and freedom is slavery! Ignorance is Strength!" the language became "newspeak", catching members in a mesh of inextricable double-talk that precluded critical thinking.

Even Benji's sense of humor altered drastically. "I didn't laugh at things I once found very funny. Everything was urgent...deadly serious. Slipping on a banana peel would have been a loss of God's time...there was *nothing* funny about it anymore." Instead his smile had become a virtual piece of jewelry, worn in public to create a good impression and help spread "God's work". Flower-selling and "witnessing" (recruiting) required boundless enthusiasm and energy, so one had to look—even feel—perpetually happy and smiling.

"Witnessing is joy, because through witnessing you can make Him (God) happy, and through fund-raising you can make Him happy," said the study guide. "You feel joy, therefore, always His joy is my joy."

Acquiring such "joy" often required diligent practice. Many members had to go through "smiling conditioning", during which they walked around with permanent smiles pasted to their faces, reinforced by the constant love and approval of the group. Often other members might stop to tickle the "smilers" to teach them how to laugh more spontaneously.

All the baggage of one's former personality had to be transferred over to the new value system; one had to laugh, smile, cry and fear when God required it, not when the individual did. In the meantime, you simply went through the motions, hoping that one day the new "God-centred" feelings would fill in.

As more and more of Benji's old concepts fell by the wayside, he could more easily identify the remaining "weaknesses". Two of the hardest to overcome were the "concepts" of hunger and fatique, which gave him constant difficulty. As little as he ate, there was always a stronger brother who ate less, as early as he woke, there was always a stronger sister up first—underscoring his weakness and pushing him to drive still harder.

"I will try to challenge the limits of time, ability and effort today," said a tiny card he carried in his pocket, and he repeated this pledge three times a day.

Another difficult problem that haunted him and most other members was the unmentionable one—lust—referred to euphemistically as a "Chapter 2 problem" (the chapter of Divine Principle dealing with sex as original sin). "It was the most evil thought of all, as horrible as death to contemplate...but one of the hardest to stifle," remembers Benji. Sometimes when he was recruiting, a woman would pass by and lust would suddenly attack, so Benji would have to exert all his will power to "turn the concept around in my head".

"I'd track down the concept—namely that I found the woman attractive. Then I'd substitute a new thought immediately, telling myself she was God's child...and I had to bring her closer to God. Then I'd chant it out until a new, dull kind of feeling would start to well up in me and then suddenly—Bang!—I'd just SWITCH ideas. The old feeling would be gone."

However, the "concept" that gave Benji by far the most difficulty, was his old "conscience". Now that he was God's agent, working to save mankind at this crucial juncture in history, his mission was urgent: he had to bring people and money away from the Satanic world and toward God's Truth—a task so important that old concepts of "truth" crumbled before it.

When selling flowers, members would often pass themselves off as anything from private businessmen to senior citizen volunteers. Similarly they would cut the stems off three-day old flowers to make them appear fresh, and some members even had short-changing down to a science. "It didn't matter what you did. It was only Satan's money...and we were bringing it over to God.

"That was my big weakness," recalls Benji. "I had a hard time conning old people, cripples—anyone who looked like they could use the money badly. It really went against my grain.

"But by the later months, I had already convinced myself that the reservations I had were *my* problems, my limited concepts...and I had to have the discipline to resolve them. Intellectually I knew that I was offering people a thread to God by getting them to give us money. It was only a question of learning to live up to my ideals."

During his last month of flower-selling, Benji was walking down a back street, when an elderly woman keeled over in front of him and struck her head on the pavement, blood trickling slowly from her mouth. For a while the Benji of old emerged, as he rushed into a nearby restaurant, grabbed a tablecloth off a table, and went back to comfort the still unconscious woman. He called a hospital and spent an hour nursing her back to consciousness, until the ambulance finally arrived.

When the woman had been carried away, Benji dutifully reported the incident to his flower team leader, expecting to be commended. Instead he was rebuked for wasting God's time when he should have been fund-raising. "Let the dead bury the dead!" his team leader snapped.

"At first, a part of me reacted against it...the first time the old me had come out so heavily in months," recalls Benji. "I felt I was right! Then, slowly, as I centred on it, I began to see, and substitute a new concept. The old woman *was* a part of the evil world, and I hadn't helped her get any closer to God. Instead I had wasted an hour of God's time that could have been used to bring in funds that were crucial to the Mission.

"Helping the old woman had been following my old concepts...old, small concepts I had decided to rid myself of...I felt very, very guilty and realized I had done the *wrong thing,* and couldn't let it happen again. I had a mission, God's mission...and it was far too important to stop for anyone. LET THE DEAD BURY THE DEAD!"

12

It was not until the end of Benji's second month with the Project that he finally "accepted" Reverend Moon as Father. In the weeks leading up to it, Benji had been living in a special house for early members in San Francisco, where Moon's name had come up more and more frequently during daily lectures about great philosophers and psychologists. Films and literature also made increasingly common mention of Moon, until it became clear to Benji and other recruits that he was somehow "associated" with the Project.

Simultaneously, religious indoctrination had evolved into a historical theory demonstrating that "Godless communism" was on the march throughout the world, and that a Messiah, much like Buddha or Jesus, was already somewhere on earth, ready to change the course of human history and win mankind back to God.

Information on the Messiah and Moon began to dovetail in the later weeks, until even their dates of birth were similar. Finally Benji took the required leap of faith; and suddenly "realized" it was him. "Things had been moving in that direction for several days, the possibility growing in my mind...until, one day—Bang! I just *knew* it. No one had to tell me...no one ever does. Reverend Moon was the Messiah."

Benji's initial three-month commitment ended with hardly a passing notice. What had originally seemed a temporary decision by his weakened self to try "living up" to the group's standards had become a self-perpetuating mechanism.

Just posing the question of leaving at the end of the three months was unthinkable; to pose any question, Benji knew by then, was to question everything—the group, the Church, the very existence of God. The remaining contradictions—such as Rev. Moon's apparent wealth, or the liquor served at Aladdin's would take time to understand. But they would be understood; for now, any doubts had to be put aside.

"If there are contradictions, they are always your weakness, not Father's," said his group leaders. "You're either faithful to the new ideal, or you're not." And it was true. By the end of the fifth month in the Church, Benji had even come to accept the one new concept that he had never expected to, the one idea he had resisted throughout his indoctrination—the existence of Satan.

In the last two months Satan was an idea that had come up more and more frequently, an almost mythical figure responsible for the evil and "negativity" that plagued the world. But Benji had never taken it literally: "It was always just a sort of image.

"It was one thing to believe in God—even in a guy named Reverend Moon I'd never met, who was the Messiah—but Satan was something I just couldn't accept, even then."

Only in his final gruelling month with the Church did Benji realize that Satan was a terrifying reality. It had come to him during MFT—Mobile Fundraising Team—the most intense activity a Moonie undergoes: "Flower selling for God".

The flower mission had begun soon after his coffeeshop encounter with Marilyn and me, during our first attempt to see him in San Francisco. Only hours later, Benji was off on a suddenly announced "secret mission" to Canada where he remained the entire time we were in San Francisco waiting to see him.

That month in Canada was his most intense period of Moonie life; travelling across the Western Provinces with four other members in a van, sleeping as little as one hour a night and eating almost nothing, driving himself relentlessly in a three-week blitz that took him from the Queen Charlotte Islands off British Columbia to the town of North Battleford, Saskatchewan.

They worked the streets furiously, 18 hours a day, and the results were "Great for God". On several occasions he and a female partner made more than $1000 a day, passing themselves off as enterprising, clean-cut kids trying to get started in the business world.

In the midst of this unrelenting activity, with virtually no food or sleep, and a skin rash breaking out on his legs, Benji had finally discovered Satan. "The isolation and intensity of my life was so great that I needed some kind of support—an enemy I could hate and fear so much it would drive me harder, and keep the doubt out. Something I could blame for the pain, and the hunger and the hardships...so Satan became a reality, like it already was for the rest of the flower-selling team."

It was Satan who threw him out of bars where he tried to sell his flowers, Satan behind the drunks who hooted at him at night, Satan who tried to overcome him with sleep and hunger and the skin rash that plagued him and other members of the team as they tried to carry out God's work. It was Satan who put him to sleep at the steering wheel during all night drives to the next town.

Satan was everywhere. He ruled the entire selfish world, and he even ruled the evil concepts that still lurked deep in Benji's own mind. His own doubts and negative thoughts were no longer just weak concepts to be rid of, Benji realized; they were invasions of Satan himself, to be fought off at the price of even his life.

"The biggest Satan is you yourself, not others," said *Master Speaks*. "If we can subjugate the biggest Satan within ourselves, we can subjugate any Satan, anywhere in the world...he who can control himself, will be able to control the world."

It was no longer just guilt or idealism that motivated Benji, but sheer terror: terror that if he stopped, even for a second, Satan would steal his mind and take him back to the evil, demented existence that awaited those who abandoned God...back to a fate "worse than death".

There was God and ecstasy on one side, the horror of Satan on the other, and nothing in between, Benji realized as he raced through the streets chanting, praying and running for God. One false step and he was doomed.

"Glory to Heaven. Peace on Earth. STAMP OUT SATAN!"

As bizarre and unrecognizeable as Benji's behavior may have been he never really became the "restored personality" that he appeared to be. "Inside, I was always struggling, trying to overcome my old concepts and live up to my 'ideal' ones. That struggle was never resolved."

Like most Church members, Benji's Moonie personality was completely severed from his feelings, acting according to a set of ideas—an ideology—rather than any emotions he actually experienced. He was always doing "what I was *supposed* to be doing...not what I felt like doing."

Perhaps it is this gap between what they are doing and what they are actually feeling that accounts for the glassy, detached look that we saw on Benji. Many others have reported the look in Moonies and other cult members: a hollow, disconnected appearance that gives one the impression, in Daphne Greene's words, that "No one is at home.

"They're looking at you with a big grin and saying 'I love you!', but somehow it doesn't seem real at all...because it isn't. They're just doing what they've been programmed to do...there's no feeling behind it at all."

In time, this too would have changed, had Benji stayed with the Church long enough. Cult-watchers and ex-members all report that after one or two years in the group, the member gradually loses his "thousand-mile stare" and plastic smile and returns to an apparently genuine state, like

Bethie. It is, says one psychiatrist "like an actor who plays his role so well and so long, he becomes lost in it forever".

These Moonies make the best recruiters and the most convincing spokespeople; the ones who are thrust before the cameras and the microphones to deny charges that the Unification Church uses any form of "mind control".

Like Bethie, they are still totally obedient servants of Rev. Moon and his doctrine, but they seem to be as alive and spontaneous as anyone else.

Exactly why this transformation occurs remains a mystery, in a field that is shrouded in many mysteries; but the most likely explanation seems to be that the recruit simply grows into his new role. As a child is socialized to obey and then internalize society's complex rules, so does the Moonie learn to fill his part, by obeying first and learning to feel later.

"If you keep on repeating an expression or behavior pattern long enough," says Dr. Clark, "eventually it will be learned and internalized...just like a foreigner in the English-speaking culture learns how to laugh at the correct times, and becomes increasingly natural with Western ways and body movement.

"In time, everything about the cult member sort of shifts over and adapts to the new behavior. The old person is effectively destroyed...and the person has become a valid new personality."

Fortunately, Benji never got quite this far. Midway through his flower-selling mission, his "team" arrived in Edmonton, Alberta, to pick up their latest shipment of flowers, sent by plane from California. With the flowers came an urgent message for Benji from his sister Debbie in Montreal.

13

Three days later Benji was on a plane back to San Francisco to meet his sister and mother. He had talked to Debbie twice since receiving her message, and had reacted in typical Moonie fashion.

"It wasn't so much that I wanted to see Debbie personally, it was more of a chance to bring her over to God. She was young, bright and idealistic...we figured I'd spend a day at Washington House with her and my mother...then convince Debbie to come up to Boonville alone. God had sent her to us."

Hours after he arrived in San Francisco, Benji returned to the airport to pick up his mother and sister. Soon he was on his way to their hotel room to drop off their luggage. The kidnap that followed was a blur of events, as he was hauled from the hotel room with "a thousand things whirling through my mind."

"Part of me felt a tremendous fear. This was it—*Satan* had come to get me. But at the same time, another part of me was stunned to see everyone there—my friends, family...I remember my father standing at the back of the room, crying..."

By the time he was back at the hide-out, the Moonie part of Benji was in firm control, determined to be strong and stave off "Satan's attack".

"I didn't see you guys as real or sincere people—just agents of Satan. I was God's servant...you were plotting to steal me back to Satan. Everything was black and white."

Somewhere inside him, a part of his old concepts still tugged at him, wanted to talk to his friends and his parents, but he had been warned that "Satan works best through those you love." It would be selfish vanity to think he could possibly argue with Satan and win.

He made a "silence condition": say nothing, hear nothing and chant—to centre on God. "I had to shut you out...shut out every word that you said."

From the start of the kidnapping to Ford's arrival next day, Benji's tactics worked. Chanting continuously during every second of his waking hours, he was able to shut off his mind completely and shut out the evil appeals of those about him. "I was way above you. By the second day, I was very confident that I could outlast you...all I wanted was a chance to escape."

Everything changed when Satan arrived, in the person of Ford Greene. "When he first touched me, I was so terrified I just about had a heart attack!" Benji recalls. "His name, his face...everything about him *reeked* of evil. I was in a total state of fear from the second he walked in."

Benji sensed that Ford knew everything going on in his mind. His presence was like an electric bolt, shocking Benji off God's track. As Ford's arm draped round him, Benji was seized with utter terror, and could no longer concentrate on chanting. Without the chant to guard his mind, "all I could do was sit and listen."

Soon Benji was listening to Ford's onslaught of questions and accusations about the Church then to Virginia's quiet plea for Benji to give the "other side" a chance. Frustration at his own silence began to grow inside him, until he unexpectedly found himself talking back—and feeling "tremendous relief" at doing so.

"The minute I opened my mouth I was in trouble. As my words came out, I had the feeling they weren't really coming from inside me. They sounded more like tape recordings of something I had heard.

"I knew that I wasn't making sense...that I was starting to break down...but a part of me *wanted* to keep on talking."

Within hours of the start of the discussion, Ford's grinding questions seemed to have opened a fissure in Benji's head. He found himself asking questions he had suspended months ago, and been terrified to reconsider since.

How could "serving God" require him to con little old ladies and cripples out of their last pennies? Why did he spend so much time collecting money when the Church was trying to eliminate materialistic thinking? Did Reverend Moon really manufacture machine guns in Korea—and how could that serve "unconditional love"?

The lines of logic had once seemed so clear, but now everything had blurred...why was it all so hard to explain?

More than anything else, it was the presence of his friends and the near-presence of his parents that undermined the Moonie in Benji, invoking the contradiction between "what I felt and what I was *supposed* to feel.

"I had started off seeing you all as incredibly evil...agents of Satan. But gradually, it became harder and harder for me to see it that way. The more disorganized you seemed, the more haphazard and ridiculous your plans were, the harder it was for me to see you as part of a plot by Satan.

"It all seemed so incredibly honest...and human. You had travelled all this distance, put in all this time, money and risk...all just to talk to me. It was overwhelming."

When he heard his parents had been arrested that morning, Benji had felt "terrible...just awful. There was no way I could convince myself they were Satanic, no matter what I knew I was supposed to believe."

His old concepts were churning inside of him, boiling over the barriers of guilt and terror that held them in. It was as though there were two different people inside of him—the old Benji on the bottom, trying desperately to escape, and the Moonie on top, struggling to maintain its mental grip; as though two separate people were fighting for control of his mind and only one could survive.

"The more I believed what you were saying, the more the old part of me wanted to break out. My mind was working for the first time...it didn't want to go back to not thinking again.

"It was harder and harder for the Moonie part of me to keep the lid on...so much was happening underneath. I felt like a dam was about to burst in my head."

Lenny's tears were the final jolt. As they streamed down Lenny's cheeks and Ford stood nearby transfixed, Benji knew without a doubt that this was *not* Satan or selfishness before him—no matter what the Church said. "It was concern and love..."

And if it was, he knew, the implications were enormous ...unthinkable..."I felt a tremendous sense of momentum building inside me and I couldn't do anything to stop it. All the thoughts and feelings I had been holding back for so long just started rushing up inside me...swelling and swelling, until—POW!—the Moonie me just broke wide open, and I was flooded with a thousand different feelings."

In the very moment after this had happened, the Moonie part of Benji was suddenly there again, filled with shame and terror at his weakness, and the horrifying consequences that would follow.

"I had a horrible dread that this was *it*—I had sinned and now I would pay the price...become possessed, insane and all the other things the Church had convinced me would happen if I lost God. There was a sensation of falling...falling out of control through mid-air. It was absolutely terrifying...the most insecure moment of my life...

"And then gradually, there was this incredible sense of relief, as I started to realize that I wasn't going to hit bottom...there *was* no Satan waiting for me—just my friends, my family and *me*. The Moonie me was gone—but *I* was still there."

Not all deprogrammings are as sudden or dramatic as Benji's. According to Ford Greene and other deprogrammers, there are as many varieties of deprogramming as there are individuals in the Church, "it all depends on the person beneath the Moonie."

While Ford took a "hard-line Satan" approach because of our tense circumstances, Moonies are often left to "chant it out" until they tire of it on their own—sometimes as much as four or five days later. Some may snap out of Moonie reality as suddenly as Benji; but others may "smoulder and smoke" for hours, the Moonie identity gradually falling away "like dead skin", with no discernible breaking moment. In some cases, Church members may simply walk out of the cult on their own, and show up at a deprogrammer's home—so torn by inner conflicts that something in them pushes them to seek "outside" help.

But regardless of the circumstances surrounding them, deprogrammings are almost always extremely emotional experiences. According to Kent Burtner, an Oregon priest who has been dealing with Unification Church members for several years: "People's emotional lives don't die when they go in there; they're very much alive, but they're just corked. So there's all kinds of emotional stuff going on, and it may involve a dynamic with parents. It may involve feelings about an old relationship."

The key, says Burtner, is to "elicit some genuine emotional responses from the individual, to help him get back in touch with his own emotional life".

To Benji, Boonville's indoctrination managed to exaggerate all the negative things in his life and the world, to "make everything seem evil. Deprogramming was the opposite...it reminded me of the good things I had managed to wipe out of my mind. It reminded me of all of you and what you meant to me...that there *were* people and things of value in my old life."

"When I was in the Church I thought nothing could break me, but my weakness was you guys."

His first weeks back were the most difficult. Several California Moonies had been sent to Montreal to find him, so at his own request Benji went into hiding again. He spent the time in a tiny lakeside cottage in the Laurentian hills outside Montreal, recuperating in near-seclusion. His only company was Ford's "assistant", Virginia, who had agreed to come to Montreal to help Benji sort out his myriad questions.

"I was very fragile and felt I needed to be taken care of," recalls Benji of those first two weeks. "There was a transition period in which I had to learn to make my own decisions again. I hadn't made any decisions whatsoever for almost six months.

"I couldn't even decide the smallest things...like what to eat, or read or wear. At Boonville, *everything* had been taken care of for me."

The period of readjustment following deprogramming is generally referred to as "rehabilitation", and can last weeks or months in some cases. Returning to normal life, ex-members face a "culture shock" so extreme, one therapist compares it to "returning from another planet".

Some ex-members may even "float" back to their Moonie reality on occasion, a frightening experience that has been compared to the halluconegenic "acid flashbacks" reported by LSD users. Fortunately, Benji did not suffer this problem and readjusted quickly to his old world.

He spent most of his time in the country quietly reading "junk" literature, canoeing and discussing his experience with Virginia, "the only person who understood what I'd been through." He also started a diary as "therapy" to put himself in touch with his emotions again.

"I'd lost a connection with my own feelings. I'd spent so much time doing what I was supposed to do that I'd lost the ability to know what I wanted to do. Just taking a walk in the country with the dogs was a really special experience. In the Moonies the only way you could do that was with 50 other people.

"That time in the country was like getting reacquainted with an old friend I hadn't seen for a long time...except in this case, the old friend was me."

At the end of the two weeks, Virginia returned to California and Benji to Montreal. He found a small apartment and spent the next few weeks on his own, fixing up his flat and regaining the rest of the thirty-five pounds he had lost during his stay with the Church.

"I liked being alone...doing quiet stuff like cooking, painting and reading. I needed lots of personal space." As time went by he became more social, and began looking up old friends. In the early weeks, he was hesitant to explain his experience publicly, worried "people would think I was crazy—that only some idiot would become involved in that kind of thing".

Eventually his confidence grew, and he decided to do all he could, and "whatever people learned from it would be better than nothing at all." Since then he has given occasional lectures at high schools and community centres, and appeared on media, in hopes that he can spare other young people from learning about the Church the way he did.

He has also met numerous parents with children in cults. He tries to help them understand their child's "new world", and in one case he consoled a set of Montreal parents whose daughter was killed in a car accident, working on a Moonie Mobile Fundraising team in the U.S. He does not wish to get involved in kidnapping people he doesn't know, though he has "talked out" several cult members who agreed to see him voluntarily.

Looking back, Benji thinks he was deceived by a "remarkably clever scheme that got me believing I was in the most loving, sincere, idealistic environment in the world...when all I was really doing was giving up my personality. I see where I was becoming more and more totally obedient, and less and less human...treating people coldly and callously in the name of 'love'.

"It scares me to think what I would have been willing to do "for God" a few months later—probably even pick up a gun and go off to war for Moon in Korea."

Benji is convinced that had he been found by the Church during his deprogramming, he was sufficiently "programmed" to press charges against his own family. "The Church would have made me feel guilty about my selfishness—my small purpose—in not helping them to fight future kidnappings by setting an example. Given my perspective at the time, I'm sure I would have gone along."

For all the frightening aspects of his time with the Moonies, the experience has not left Benji pessimistic; in fact, it has strengthened his "belief in humanity".

"I felt good about the people I knew before the whole experience, but now I have even more faith in people in general and my friends in particular. I see where everyone is special in his own way, and you have to respect them for that—not for their potential to become something else. Everyone has their own unique value."

He is convinced that "there are all kinds of forces in society that want to control people and take away their individuality. The Unification Church is just one of the most extreme examples. It's ironic—a lot of people like me go into the Moonies to try and escape being limited by society's rules and controls—but they end up doing just the opposite. They get themselves locked in a deeper rut than they ever imagined could be possible."

Today Benji has completed the second year of a three year physiotherapy program at McGill University. The decision to change careers was a largely practical one, as the prospect of finding teaching jobs looks increasingly grim in Quebec. He finds it "hard work, but extremely satisfying.

"I feel quite excited about life" he says cheerfully. "I like the prospects for the future, even if a lot of things are still uncertain. I'm very confident that things will work out well for me.

"In the long run, I think I've actually gained from the Moonie experience. I understand myself and my susceptibilities better...and I think I accept the complexities of life with no delusion at all about finding any magic solutions. I guess the whole experience has taught me the danger of looking outside myself for solutions.

"The only person who can run my life is me."

Benji's deprogramming was a success, but not all have such fairy tale endings. Benji had gone into Boonville relatively untroubled, and he came out much the same way; but others who plunge into the cult to escape longstanding problems often find life equally or more difficult when they emerge.

Old relationships, career problems, guilt and anger at being taken for a sucker by the cult can all play on the ex-member, leading to severe emotional difficulties. "When you go into the Unification Church", says Burtner, "these problems go into the ice box, and when you come out, these things are going to thaw out."

Conscientious deprogrammers will often continue working with an ex-cult member long after the actual deprogramming has ended—a "rehabilitation" process that can take months, and even years, to complete. One Canadian therapist says it takes an average of an hour of therapy a week for six months before most cult members feel "liberated" from the group's influence; thus deprogramming may be only the beginning of the story.

Some deprogrammers do not take such care, and the results sometimes lead to renewed problems. The most notorious example of this approach is Ted Patrick, who claims more than 1500 deprogrammings in the past seven years. Patrick's "lightning" deprogrammings result in many instant successes, but sometimes youngsters are left behind in confusion.

Similarly, for Moonies and others immersed in a cult for several years, deprogramming can sometimes be a risky business. The longer the member remains in the cult, the more his "old concepts" get buried under an avalanche of new ones, and the higher the chance they will shrivel, rot and die.

Deprogramming at this point can sometimes leave a "pretty hollow shell," says Singer, who has seen several long-term cult members deprogrammed. "They were sociable and smiling," she recalls, "but I noticed a certain superficiality, an emptiness that remained for as long as two years afterwards."

According to Dr. John Clark, some veteran cult members, particularly those in groups that do too much chanting, may burn out their old personalities so completely that "the process becomes irreversible.

"Nothing is left when you deprogram them except a black space between the ears,' he warns. "They've been in too long and chanted too much...their minds are gone."

Most cult members who have not been in the group for too long *can* be successfully deprogrammed—often without even recourse to kidnapping. Toronto psychiatrist Saul V. Levine works with cult members who see him voluntarily. All of these are members who have been reluctantly convinced to come to Levine by their family—none of them has been kidnapped—and Dr. Levine discards the term "deprogramming". He sees it as a "very intensive conversation", and says the results are "impressive".

"But there has to be at least a tiny crack in the armor for them to have agreed to see me," he points out. "The fact that they're willing to talk means that there's already a touch of skepticism inside, even if it's only miniscule...If you can get them to ask one question, all the other ones they've repressed come rushing out."

Once members have remained in several months, however, they often become like Benji—totally unwilling to discuss or even hear the "other side". "They're closed off. With kids like that," admits Dr. Levine, "I haven't gotten to square one."

Dr. Levine is critical of forced deprogrammings like Benji's in all but the most desperate of circumstances. Like many others he feels that using force violates the cult members' civil liberties and sets a dangerous precedent for the deprogramming of other religious, and even political, groups. He has also seen the results of numerous "failed" kidnap-deprogrammings—that have resulted in emotional problems, estrangement from families and sometimes a return to the cult.

He has heard of some successes like Benji's, but overall Dr. Levine says bluntly that he is "not impressed...with the process, the people who do it, or the results."

Yet for all of his misgivings about kidnapping, Dr. Levine understands the painful dilemma of parents faced with the "overwhelming power" of some cults.

"Something like Jonesville makes you think again," he acknowledges. "If any parent of a young person in Jonesville had considered deprogramming prior to the holocaust there, they might have saved their lives. Much as I don't agree with it, I can sympathize with a parent who just doesn't want to take that chance."

Deprogramming is a tremendously complex issue, with no clear-cut answers. Unquestionably, cults with the psychological hold of the Moonies are a frightening phenomenon, with grave and possibly lasting effects on those they entrap. It is not hard to understand those who would like to send an army of deprogrammers into the many Boonvilles in North America, to end the problem of cults "once and for all".

Yet force is rarely more than a temporary solution, that addresses symptoms rather than genuine ills. Just as the Moonies err in clasping onto a single, simple solution to the infinite cross-currents of life, it would be a mistake to see deprogramming as an instant solution to the complex problem of cults.

Deprogramming is a tool—an extraordinary one that can sometimes work "miracles" like Benji's—but it is not the real answer. That answer lies in understanding the soil in which cults such as the Moonies grow.

14

Trying to comprehend Benji's experience is a bit like peering into a black hole in space: the deeper you look, the more unfathomable it becomes. The only time you can really understand it is when you are already being sucked into it; and by then, it is difficult to escape.

Moonie reality is so foreign to most current North American life that it will never really make sense to one who inhabits our own world. But like a black hole, we can learn something about it by studying the elements on its periphery.

A good starting point is modern psychotherapy. The general goal of most psychotherapists is to help people get "in touch" with themselves; to have them understand the relationship between their outward behavior and their inner thoughts and feelings. For instance, a depressed young medical student might examine whether he really wants to become a doctor, or whether he is only living up to the expectations of others.

Most traditional therapies operate slowly. They use increasingly personal conversations to gradually open up the patient to his own feelings, in a process that may take months or even years. But in recent years, several new therapies have produced more sudden and dramatic results by "heating up" the therapy environment. Techniques such as those of encounter groups create highly-charged emotional situations in which people's defences break down quickly, bringing them to a point where they see their behavior more clearly and are often highly vulnerable to change.

This "moment of truth" can sometimes be frightening. Some of the newer therapies have come under criticism, because rapid destruction of "defence mechanisms" may have dangerous results: some patients may suffer psychotic breakdowns, and others may become so desperate they go through near-religious conversions, endowing the therapist with magical powers.

Consequently there is a tremendous burden on the therapist in these situations: he must make sure that the environment remains supportive, and that the patient looks to himself for the solution to his problems, not to the "all-knowing" therapist.

"The purpose of psychotherapy is to help the patient to be more independent," says Dr. Terry Wilson of Rutgers University. "Everything in our training has been aimed at teaching us how to be supportive...to allow the patient to come to the insights *himself.*"

It is at this point that psychotherapy and Moonie indoctrination move in exactly opposite directions. Like some kinds of therapy, Boonville creates an intense emotional environment that pushes the "patient" into the recesses of his own mind. In fact, Boonville is far more intense than any recognized therapy, since the recruit is totally isolated from the real world for days on end—food and sleep are cut back; the routine is bizarre and unsettling; and throughout, the recruit does not even know he is undergoing a "therapy" experience.

As a result, many recruits break down quickly, coming to a volatile and vulnerable state that is sometimes the object of intense therapies. However, at this point, it is as if the "therapist" has gone mad: rather than pulling back to help the patient find answers in himself, the Moonies close in, deliberately using the recruit's growing vulnerability to drive him to the very brink of a nervous breakdown. Then, as he teeters in terror on the fringes of sanity, he is offered only one refuge to avoid going insane: abandoning his own identity entirely and fastening onto the "benevolent therapist" to lead him to safety.

The therapy process has been perverted to achieve exactly what responsible therapy labors to avoid—the creation of a total, God-like dependence on the "therapist" as the only barrier between the recruit and madness. The love and support of the group around him (the Moonies) is now the only defence against the recruit's inner terror. Worse yet, once this has been achieved, the group then systematically turns this awesome power back upon the weakened recruit to dismember and obliterate all remnants of his former identity.

In the weeks ahead, the recruit is convinced that he has lived a hopelessly selfish existence: the only way out of his horrifying plight is to annihilate his old personality and rebuild it from scratch at the "therapist's" directions. This is never stated explicitly, but it is understood: from this point onwards, the recruit may trust only the group's standards—rigorous and strange as they may seem—and not his own ego-centred perspective. Whatever experience, knowledge and emotions that previously guided his behavior are worth nothing in the days ahead. They are "old concepts" that he must be strong enough to subdue.

This is the crucial juncture in becoming a Moonie; it is at this point that whatever makes up the person's identity is totally invalidated, blotted out of any role in determining his future path. The recruit has been so terrified that he has lost all confidence in his own thoughts and feelings to guide his actions. To be accepted, he is ready to disbelieve *everything* he thinks and feels and obey *anything* the group tells him: a state of such utter submission that, like Benji, recruits can be steered not just off the path—but in the very opposite direction to that in which they had intended to go.

A desire for more freedom is used to lead them into slavery; an ache to express more love for humanity is turned into hatred for all but a few; and a yearning to liberate their potential from society's restrictions is used to transform them into fossilized zombies, with almost no spontaneous behavior remaining.

As grotesque as this metamorphosis may be, the power that fuels it is not new: it is obedience, in its purest form—not because the recruit fears authority, but because he has no confidence whatever in his own worth. The only thing that now gives his life meaning is the love and respect of the group—and the group will love him only so long as he continues to obey them.

In the apt words of Dr. Robert Jay Lifton, a psychoanalyst who has studied the effects of "brainwashing" for more than 20 years: "Self comes to depend on authority for its very existence. 'I exist, therefore I am' has been transformed into 'I obey, therefore I am.' "

This total annihilation of self-worth and utter willingness to obey is the very essence of the Unification Church's control over its members. It is why the Church appears to exercise "mind-control"—because in a sense the person's behavior is no longer directed by his own mind. He is discounting all his own thoughts, feelings and values as "inner enemies" and acting entirely at the direction of an outside authority. He no longer trusts himself. And it is very scary, because we can see it at work in the glassy expression of many early members, like Benji, so obviously detached from their inner emotions. They look like puppets on psychological strings. They sound like "opinionated robots". We know that they will obey anything they are told and we wonder how far they would go, if asked.

This absolute authority the Moonies exercise over their members is the basis of their cult's power. Yet while the Unification Church may acquire and use this weapon more ferociously and systematically than others, it is by no means its sole proprietor. This same "giving up" of thoughts, feelings and values to an external authority can be found to varying degrees in a number of areas of human life.

To begin with, not surprisingly, we can see it at play to

some extent in other North American cults. Few, if any, pursue it as relentlessly as the Moonies; in some groups, the degree of control seems far less marked; but it appears to be a theme common to the control techniques of almost all.

Many North American "spiritual masters", from teenage gurus to aging yogis, routinely demand that their disciples obey even the most bizarre and "nonsensical" of commands; members must assume that all contradictions stem from their lack of knowledge rather than the master's possible imperfection. Thus Guru Maharaj Ji and Rev. Moon can live in luxury, and other "spiritual leaders" can flirt with drugs and women while their emaciated members live in barren poverty, passing off their own lack of comprehension as an inner weakness. "Everything is my inadequacy, not Master's...Later I will understand."

In the meantime, these young members must construct endless rationalizations to explain away contradictions, as with one disciple of Guru Maharaj Ji, who told me: "It's true that Maharaj Ji drives fancy cars and drinks liquor...but that's because he is already perfect. He isn't corrupted by material things like you or me..."

Implicit in all these mental contortions is the same message: I cannot trust my own feelings or thoughts, because I am hopelessly inadequate. "The family would always tell us 'What's inside your mind is lies'," reports one former member of the Love Family, a cult on the U.S.Pacific Coast. "We are your mind. The group is your mind."

Guru Maharaj Ji also pulls no punches in this hypnotic Satsang lecture, explicitly telling his disciples:

"So whatever you have got, give it to me. I am ready to receive it. And the extra thing you have got is your mind. Give it to me. I am ready to receive it. Because your mind troubles you, give it to me. It won't trouble me. Just give it. And give your egos to me because egos trouble you, but they don't trouble me. Give them to me."

According to Ted Patrick all cults gain their authority by getting the members to hate or distrust their inner thoughts.

"They *all* use the same set of techniques to turn their members into zombies," says Patrick. "The cult teaches you to hypnotize yourself. It tells you that your mind is evil...that thinking is the machinery of the devil...like being stabbed in the heart with a dagger. Then it tells you that you are supposed to use your mind only to serve God—and God is always the leader."

Patrick may be excessive in his blanket statement, but certainly many cults use this form of control to some extent—ranging from the benign degree of some yogis to the near-total control of the Unification Church. I am not familiar with enough cults to enumerate and differentiate them—but a consumer guide to the relative "obedience index" of various North American groups might prove a valuable contribution to existing cult literature.

It is important to note however, that not all so-called fringe groups in North America necessarily encourage members to distrust their own thinking and feeling processes. Traditional Zen Buddhism, for instance, is a strongly anti-authoritarian movement that calls upon its disciples to use their own strength, mind and experience to guide them before all else. "One has to walk the path of enlightenment alone," is the essential message of this religion. "All a teacher can do is provide the occasional signpost along the journey."

Buddha is the "enlightened one," but he speaks in the name of a person's own wisdom, not in the name of an allpowerful supernatural force. Consequently, members are encouraged to use their *own* senses to interpret the world around them; to see that no knowledge is of any value unless it grows of themselves. Serious Zen Buddhism is not a form of mind control, though some individual cult leaders may use such techniques in the name of Zen.

Conversely, just as groups sometimes perceived as cults do not eradicate inner values, others which are not seen as cults sometimes do.

Ehrard Seminar Training (EST) for example, is a modern "group therapy" popular in California, and would not be considered a cult. Its initiates continue to live ordinary, individual lives upon "graduating", and EST claims members such as actress Valerie Harper and singer John Denver.

Yet certain similarities between EST and the Unification Church are at least unnerving. EST too gains its members through an intensive "group experience"—two successive weekend seminars that are sold as "60 hours that transform your life". People are warned in advance that EST is going to "tear you apart, and put you back together again". The weekends are spent essentially locked in a hotel ballroom with 250 people (at $300 a head) for 18 hours a day, during which participants are permitted only limited bathroom and food breaks—determined by EST trainers.

Some people reportedly urinate in their pants. Participants are harangued, confronted and verbally assaulted by EST trainers who tell them they are "turkeys" and "assholes". At the peak of the second weekend, as their defences are battered down, many participants fall to the ground sobbing and crying, some shouting "I've got it! I've got it!"

What EST graduates appear to "get" is a theme similar to that sold in many cults. Their identities have been pried open, then stuffed full at the crucial moment with the EST philosophy: everyone is responsible for his own life, and whatever befalls them must have been "created" by them. This has reportedly led at least one EST graduate to state that raped women wanted to be raped, Vietnamese babies wished to be napalmed and Jewish concentration camp victims desired to be exterminated.

Others have reported that their pasts are just "troublesome tapes" that must be completely shut out of their minds. On accepting the new "philosophy" (along with the love and acceptance of their fellow graduates) EST graduates often report that they have been liberated from feelings of "shame, blame and guilt". To others, however, it seems they have found a perfect way to shut off their conscience: if they feel guilt about living well while others are in want they shouldn't—it is not their responsibility. Those who are suffering have "created" their own problems.

The EST philosophy is relatively innocuous and even seems helpful to some people; one could argue that it is just a psychic booster shot of the system's current values—getting people to enjoy their good fortune while putting other people's misfortune out of mind. Another West Coast operation called Gideon has recently gone a step further, offering a similar "training program" to those who feel pangs of conscience at inheriting large sums of money.

After a weekend of EST-style training, Gideonites suddenly "get" that it makes sense to inherit great wealth without guilt or obligation. Wealth is suddenly seen as "inherited talent", and any qualms have been abolished from the mind.

Neither EST nor Gideon is to be compared with the Moonies. These groups control people for only a weekend, then allow them to go home (though "booster sessions" may be taken regularly). Participants are warned in advance of what they will undergo. But the underlying process of breaking down one's inner values and sense of identity in order to replace them with those of an outside party, however comforting it may be, is similar enough to be disturbing. And one wonders how much control EST could gain over its "graduates", if its techniques became more intensive and its leaders had more malevolent goals.

Yet this potential for giving up one's values to an outside authority may have a wider application than cults and a few "weird" therapies. Some people believe that the same loss of identity can afflict entire nations, if historical conditions create a national mood of confusion and despair.

In *The True Believer,* Eric Hoffer argues that mass movements often exhibit this characteristic of "stripping the person of his distinctedness and autonomy...turning (him) into an anonymous particle with no will and no judgement of its own." If information is sealed off during periods of national confusion, Hoffer believes, people become frightened, insecure and ripe to dissolve their identities in an authoritarian movement whose only credo is *ours is not to reason why, ours is but to do and die.*

At least two 20th century novelists, George Orwell and Arthur Koestler, have been haunted by a similar spectre. Writing in the wake of Stalinist Russia and Nazi Germany, both authors saw the potential for totalitarian leaders or ideologies to obliterate an individual's capacity for conscience and thought. The scenarios they envisioned bear an eerie resemblance to Benji's and other descriptions of Moonie life. Many ex-Moonies have noticed the similarities.

In *1984*, Orwell imagined a society resting on the belief that Big Brother was omnipotent and the ruling party infallible. All activity was directed at glorifying and perpetuating the Party, while the greatest offence was *thoughtcrime*—critical or negative thoughts about Big Brother or the state.

To resist this inner danger, citizens were taught a mental technique known as *crimestop*—"the faculty of stopping short as though by instinct at the threshold of dangerous thought". Similarly, all *goodthinkers* were expected to have "no private emotions" and no respite from enthusiasm, cheering and laboring for the Party. There was to be no spare time, no time alone: a taste for solitude, "even a walk by yourself" was individualistic and dangerous. There was even a name for it: *ownlife*.

The book was fictional, written in 1949, but the eradication of individual thought and feeling that Orwell warned of bears striking similarity to Moonie life. So too do the rewards the citizens of 1984 received in exchange: a sense of belonging to a great, immortal movement that was fighting to save mankind. "If he can make complete, utter submission, if he can escape from his identitiy," wrote Orwell, "if he can merge himself in the Party so that he *is* the Party, then he is all-powerful and immortal."

Arthur Koestler, was similarly frightened by the bloody turn that Stalinism took, and the blind eye turned by millions of revolutionaries—including himself, when he was a member of the Communist Party. His novel, *Darkness at Noon,* is a veiled commentary on where unbending allegiance to the Stalinist "line" was taking Russia. Again, the psychology described is more than reminiscent of Benji's state of mind.

The tragic hero of the novel is the old Bolshevik, Rubashov, who has spent his whole life deliberately repressing his inner emotions and conscience as "bourgeois sentiments"—selfish sentimentality—so he could serve the Party faithfully at every bloody turn in the revolutionary road. Sitting in his cell awaiting execution at the end of the novel, Rubashov's mind is flooded by silent memories of friends and lovers he has ruthlessly betrayed over the years, "for the good of the cause".

Yet to the end, Rubashov is still so grafted to the ideology of the Party that he cannot accept these memories as valid, or even as part of himself. Self does not exist. Even the word "I" has no meaning for Rubashov: he refers to it instead as "the grammatical fiction".

"The I (was) a suspect quality. The Party did not recognize its existence. The definition of the individual was: A multitude of one million, divided by one million."

In a recent work, *The Nazis and the Occult,* Dusty Sklar examines the same theme of "loss of self" to explain how millions of Nazi members could change in just a few years from "ordinary citizens to mass murderers".

Sklar traces the Nazi's *Kadavergehorsam*—"cadaver obedience"—to the party's roots in German mystical society, where members gave themselves up to their teachers and "obeyed even the most eccentric commands, whether or not these commands do violence to one's conscience".

Stepping into a vacuum of social disintegration, Hitler took absolute control over the arts, literature and the news media; then with ceaseless propaganda, torch-light parades and fiery speeches, he was able to heat up Germany's emotional climate to near-religious fervor. "To many Nazis," says

Sklar, "Hitler became a Messiah, leading them in a holy cause...pathological blindness convinced them that they were participating in the superhuman task of ridding the world of a menace."

This menace was the Jew, a Satanic figure to whom Hitler attributed evil qualities that included conscience, intellect and intelligence—which held the German people back from becoming the predator *Ubermensch*. "Will" had to triumph over conscience in the New Germany.

"The intellect has grown autocratic and has become a disease of life," Hitler said. "Conscience is a Jewish invention. It is a blemish, like circumcision." Instead Hitler would teach the German people to develop the "will": he would create a German youth before whom the world would "shrink back".

"There must be no weakness or tenderness in it. I want to see once more in the eyes the gleam of pride and independence of the beast of prey...in this way I shall eradicate the thousand years of human domestication."

To help eradicate their bourgeois conscience, young Nazis were sent to Boonville-type training camps, isolated from the real world, and cut off from the influence of their parents. There they were kept busy from day to night, working, marching and marching: in former commander Hermann Rauschning's words: "Marching diverts men's thoughts. Marching kills thought, Marching makes an end to individuality."

At the camps, youngsters were subjected to a "hate" training that included ripping the eyes out of cats with "utter indifference to sorrow" to steel them in pitilessness. Similarly those sent to work as executioners in concentration camps were continually told to regard their work as sacrifice—as though any pangs of guilt one felt were not due to the crime, but rather the price one had to pay to cleanse the nation of its inner weakness.

Erich Fromm has a similar theme in *Escape from Freedom*, his psychological analysis of fascism in Germany. He too sees a messianic, religious base to the strength of the Nazi movement and a willingness to overcome one's moral code to serve a "higher" one. He links it to other mass movements.

"Where the State or the Race or the Socialist Fatherland or the Fuhrer is the object of worship," concludes Fromm, "the life of the individual becomes insignificant, and *man's worth consists in the very denial of his worth and strength.*" (My italics.)

In short, a member of a fanatic movement like the Nazis is judged—like Benji—on how well he can repress his personal thoughts and feelings: the more he succeeds in burying his self and his conscience, the "stronger and more generous" he will be considered by the movement. Strength is ability to overcome conscience.

The result of this logic was a breed of men who could say, as did one young soldier testifying at Nuremburg: "I saw women and children killed, but I did not pay attention to it. I have no opinion: I obey." Or as Hermann Goering did: "I have no conscience. Adolf Hitler is my conscience."

These were men who Hitler could boast were not only uniform in ideas, but "even the facial expression is almost the same. Look at these laughing eyes, these fanatical enthusiasms, and you will discover how a hundred thousand men in a movement become a single type."

Yet one does not have to go to Nazi Germany, or 1984, to find symptoms of this disease: its germs can be found right here in North America, where most people take their right to "be themselves" for granted—yet often willingly sacrifice it to those in authority.

War is generally the easiest time to see this process at work. During the heated emotional climate of war, many ordinarily peaceful people are easily convinced that "national purpose" calls upon all good men to support their country "right or wrong". Those who opposed the Vietnam War during the 1960's and fled their country were branded "traitors" because they could not obey orders that their conscience told them were an inhuman attack on the Vietnamese people. Yet thousands of other Americans who marched obediently off to fight the "Communist menace" (and tens of thousands of parents who sacrificed their children) were applauded as patriots for a war that later proved to have been based at least partly on presidential deceit.

At what point does conscience become treason? When must one's inner values be stifled in the name of authority?

Even in peacetime there are strong indications that the same submissive mentality is latent in North Americans. The need to obey authority is hammered into us from an early age on this continent—often regardless of whether that authority is right or not. Foreign policy is something we must generally go along with, because "we don't know all the facts". Doctors, lawyers, parents, and teachers must be obeyed because they have titles—even if one suspects they are wrong.

There is evidence to suggest that people become far more accustomed to obeying authority automatically than many of us suspect. Perhaps the most striking example of this is Stanley Milgram's famous experiment on obedience in America.

In this experiment, randomly selected people were asked to help test the effect of punishment on learning. On arriving at the elegant Yale University laboratory, they were introduced to another volunteer—a likeable middle-aged man who was then strapped into an "electric chair" contraption, while the first person was led to the adjacent room.

There he was faced with a control panel with 30 levers, beginning at 15 volts and going up to 450 volts, graded from "slight shock" through "very strong shock", through "danger: severe shock" up to the last levers, marked simply XX. A stern-faced scientist instructed him to ask questions via intercom to the "learner" in the other room, with the response to be flashed on a panel in the control booth. Every time the "learner" made a wrong response, the person in the booth was to increase the shock one level.

The person did not know that the man in the electric chair was a plant, and was not being shocked; yet all the subjects continued to give what they thought were real shocks up to 300 volts.

At that point, no answer appeared on the control panel and there was a frantic pounding on the wall of the room in which the "learner" was presumably bound to the electric chair. If the person turned to the scientist for guidance, he was coldly instructed to ignore the pounding and treat the lack of a response as a wrong answer.

After the 315-volt shock was administered, the pounding on the wall was repeated, and then there were no further sounds and no more answers on the panel. Despite the ominous silence that followed, an astonishing 26 of the 40 subjects tested continued to administer shocks to the victim past the "Danger" marking and into the XX levers. During this time, most of the subjects were observed to sweat, tremble, stutter, bite their lips, groan and dig their fingernails into their flesh. In a number of cases, they even showed signs of "bizarre" nervous laughter.

Said one stunned observer who watched the proceedings through a one-way mirror: "I observed a mature and initially poised businessman enter the laboratory smiling and confident. Within 20 minutes he was reduced to a twitching, stuttering wreck, who was rapidly approaching a point of nervous collapse. He constantly pulled on his earlobe, and twisted his hands. At one point he pushed his fist into his forehead and muttered: 'Oh God, let's stop it.' And yet he continued to respond to every word of the experimenter, and obeyed to the end."

Milgram's experiment underlines the same frightening principle at work in North American life: many people appear to be so conditioned that under pressure they will obey authority automatically—even where it clearly contradicts their own feelings and conscience. It offers an unnerving vision of just how far many might be willing to follow under stress.

Why? Why does a society that prides itself on its freedom still produce so many people ready to sacrifice the right to be themselves? Why do people so often lose their sense of integrity and conviction when placed under pressure? And what, if any, relationship does this have to the mushrooming number of cults in North America?

In recent years, a variety of books have been written on the increasingly sophisticated tools of propaganda in use, in particular for "brainwashing"—or otherwise altering the personality of individuals.

Rape of the Mind, by Joost Meerloo, *Propaganda* by Jacques Ellul, and *Techniques of Persuasion* by J.A.C. Brown are among a growing literature on the subject of how people are influenced and shaped by propaganda and psychological techniques. *Snapping,* by Flo Conway and Jim Siegelman, is a recent addition which looks specifically at "personality transformation" in contemporary cults.

All come to similar conclusions as to why indoctrination techniques are so easily able to take control of peoples' personalities and alter them. They suggest it is because we are *already* so accustomed to being controlled and altered by the forces of authority in our own society, that we do not have the inner resources to resist a "brainwashing" attack.

As Meerloo writes in *Rape of the Mind:*

"Although there is a horrifying fascination in the idea that our mental resistance is relatively weak, that the very quality which distinguishes one man from another—the individual I—can be profoundly altered by psychological pressures, such transformations are merely extremes of a process we find operating in normal life."

As these studies point out, the process of control begins in early childhood, where there is enormous pressure on youngsters to follow traditional routes of behavior. Despite some changes, much of public school is intent on training children to do what they are supposed to—teaching them to memorize meaningless facts, obey the rules and generally "fit in".

At home, many families provide similar training. With the child's interests at heart, parents may hammer home time-worn norms about the kind of spouse, friends and job one should have to live a "successful" life. Attempts by the child to break away in independent directions may be discouraged through strict rules or oppressive guilt. "Don't be different...play it safe" is a common parental theme.

In his studies of brainwashing victims in the Korean War and other situations, Meerloo found that those educated under strict rules of obedience and conformity broke down more easily under pressure of a mental attack. Training to conform served people well while they were in their own society—but undermined their inner strength and ability to adapt once those traditional supports were gone. Under pressure, Meerloo concluded, these people often welcomed the relief of an authority figure. They were used to having decisions made for them.

Psychiatrist Margaret Singer draws conclusions that are quite similar in her interviews with youngsters who fell into cults: in many of these cases, she notes, parents had often "wiped out interest in the kids' own needs and choices...

"For instance, the child may have wanted to become a botanist...and he had a real beginning of talent at it, but the parent thought that being a lawyer or a dentist was far more important. So they discouraged his enthusiasm for botany and pushed him toward law...and pretty soon he was unenthusiastic about botany, but not really committed to law. So he was no place at all when a cult member approached him...

"I find this sort of thing very common among kids who fall into cults...in all kinds of areas—friends, jobs, opinions. The ones who don't fall in are often those whose parents endorsed certain of their choices, and made them feel secure in who *they* were...made them feel confident about being *themselves.*"

The grip of parent and school authorities has been loosened somewhat in recent years. But new forces have emerged—what Fromm calls "anonymous authorities" —that similarly discourage people from learning to think and act for themselves. We live in a period where advertising, fashion, television and the corporate ethic assault people with messages of what acceptable behavior is—pressing them to conform to these standards. There is tremendous pressure on every individual to follow certain roles, regardless of how he or she feels inside.

Fashion and advertising—which Meerloo terms "the art of making people dissatisfied with what they have"—bombard us with messages of how and what we should drink, drive, dress, smoke and smell of, in order to be accepted. Television news gives the same information to all of us, at the same time and in the same order, making it more likely we will develop the same opinions, no matter how much we protest they are our own. We even learn from canned laughter what we are supposed to find funny.

These forces may guide and subtly control a youngster, undermining his ability to think for himself, as much as the more obvious authorities of past generations. Despite more permissive attitudes, few kids are encouraged to figure things out for themselves, to make choices and develop their own personalities. Often, they are simply filled up with the values of the society around them.

"Everywhere," writes Ellul in *Propaganda,* "we find men who pronounce as highly personal truths what they have read in the paper only an hour before and whose beliefs are only the result of a powerful propaganda. Everywhere we find people who have a blind confidence in a political party, a general, a movie star, a country or a cause, and who will not tolerate the slightest challenge to that God. Everywhere we meet people who...are no longer capable of making the simplest moral or intellectual distinctions, or engaging in the most elementary reasoning...we meet this alienated man at every turn, and are possibly already one ourselves."

Perhaps people who can think independently of the society

around them have never been very common—but rarely has this ability been so essential as today. In the past, a young person emerging from childhood entered a relatively close-knit society that was largely supportive of the way he or she had been raised. Traditional, expectations of a spouse, a job and a way of life made available choices limited and relatively simple—without much need for independent thought. Barring disaster, the culture around him would undergo few major changes during his lifetime; if it did, he could rely on the traditional models set by religion, family, government and other institutions to help him adapt.

Today, this is much less true. Long-standing traditions and authorities around which people used to model their lives have lost respect and weakened under the pressure of rapid change and information. The family, traditional sex roles, the work ethic, government and other models have lost much of their legitimacy, while newer ones do not seem to have emerged to replace them. People are without roots.

Today, on reaching his teens, a person is thrust into a chaotic world of multiple choices and varied lifestyles, a galaxy of ideas and identities. Will I work? At what? Will I marry...have children? are among a thousand questions that assail him from every side.

He is like a shopper in a gigantic supermarket. If he knows what he is looking for, the choice can be stimulating; but if not, the choice only serves to confuse and threaten him —pulling him from one product to the next by the color and attractiveness of the packaging alone.

Worse still, the packages on the shelf keep changing. What is in one day may be out the next; what is acceptable dress, language or behavior may be out of style soon after. Even the trade or profession he chooses may become obsolete. No sooner does a youngster begin to grasp and develop one identity then tastes shift, and he must adapt to another —changing clothes, jobs, opinions and manner as fast as current fads dictate.

And he must change with these fads, because he has never

learned how to think for himself: his only real sense of identity is his ability to fit in with those around him.

"It gets so that you're doing what's expected of you all the time, gradually losing parts of yourself to the society around you," says one young acquaintance of mine, a successful marketing executive of 30. "You start dressing like you're supposed to, acting like you're supposed to, buying what you're supposed to...all to create the right image. You don't decide...society decides and you just go along...or else you'll stick out like a sore thumb.

"Even your conscience has to start changing to fit in with the corporate conscience, if you want to get ahead. It gets so that taking advantage of people is normal. You're doing things you could never have imagined yourself doing a couple of years earlier—but eventually, you fall so far behind it all that you start losing touch with what it was you used to feel...

"You don't even know who you are anymore...only who you're expected to be. You can work to become that—maybe even make it, like I'm doing—and that gives you a certain satisfaction. But it's an empty satisfaction...something is always missing."

Not only those in the corporate world may feel such pangs of emptiness. It afflicts us all to some extent—from the obvious "seekers" ever in search of new lifestyles, to the suburban housewife, swallowing pills to avoid thinking of her real problems. Even those who rebel against society's ill are not immune: some may march with protestors, vehement about what they do not want, but unsure of what they do. "Different strokes" may mask the same problem.

Yet as society grows ever more complex, as its major institutions seem to "work" less and less, as our lack of inner strength becomes more and more apparent, many people are showing the strain. Often a personal setback, such as the loss of a job, may send us into long depressions, provoking an "identity crisis" that is the consequence of people looking inwards after years without practice.

Others sense germs of the same disease before crisis sets in, and turn to various forms of therapy—trying to get in touch with their inner thoughts and desires—hoping to learn who they are and what they want, before it is too late. If they are lucky, and find responsible help, they may eventually find some balance in their lives.

But others, far less fortunate, fall into the hands of cults, or cult-like groups, that seem to offer a similar path to self-discovery—but really have violent intent. They artfully create a therapy-like environment, and use it to confront an individual with powerful inner questions he has not squarely faced before: Who are you? What are you doing with your life? And most importantly...is this what you *really* want?

These can be valuable questions for a person to ask, if he is ready for them and if the environment is supportive: if friends, tradition and love are there to fall back on should trouble arise. But instead, these questions are presented in a Boonville environment—an isolated, foreign atmosphere that is deliberately orchestrated to drive the individual toward a crisis he is not equipped to handle.

And as many like Benji have painfully learned, the crisis can then be savagely manipulated toward whatever end the "therapist" intends.

What amazes us about the Moonie techniques is the sophistication and brutality of the attack they launch on personality, and the rapidity with which it is completed: they manage to transform a person radically in only weeks, or even days. But underlying the extremity of their methods may be many clues as to how our own society gradually represses and controls personality while it is still in its growth stages.

In the words of former Unification Church leader Alan Tate Wood: "To some extent, we have all compromised much of our spontaneity to the outside world. The unique thing about a Moonie is that he is so *completely* disassociated from his real self. There is practically nothing spontaneous about him...and that allows us to see the process much more clearly."

In this light, perhaps cults do not grow simply out of our society's weaknesses but are at the same time a projection of where those weaknesses may lead us—a macabre but revealing caricature of where our lack of control over our own lives may lead. Perhaps they warn us that the lack of inner strength and firm sense of identity fostered by our society may be the psychological material out of which blind obedience to a person, cause or country can be fashioned in times of crisis.

In a sense, the Boonville environment acts like a giant psychological bunsen burner: it heats up the unconscious fears and doubts of an individual within it until they boil over, threatening him with the terrifying existential question: If I am not who I think I am, then who am I? But it is possible that economic and social factors can transform an entire nation into a heated Boonville-type environment in which collective fears and doubts similarly rise to the surface.

If North America's social climate were to become more chaotic and uncertain under the pressure of historical and economic forces, could large numbers of people similarly lose hold of their fragile sense of security and self? As unemployment, inflation and chaos wreaked havoc on patterns of life that had been taken for granted, would many people begin to question their own values and sense of identity? And under such collective fear could they, like individuals at Boonville, seek to assuage their terror by binding to an authoritarian leader who promised an all-powerful solution to their problems?

In *Rape of the Mind* Meerloo sees just such a danger for the Western world. He warns that "If the complexity of a country's political and economic apparatus makes the individual citizen feel powerless, confused and useless, if he has no sense of participation in the forces that govern his daily life, or if he feels these forces to be so vast and confusing that he can no longer understand them, he will grasp at the totalitarian opportunity for belonging, for participation, for a simple formula that explains and rationalizes what is beyond his comprehension.''

Both he and Erich Fromm argue that the rise of the Nazi movement in Germany was at least partly a psychological reaction to economic and social disintegration: inflation and unemployment were rising, destroying traditional concepts of thrift and savings; traditional authorities were confused and discredited causing parents and government figures to lose respect in the eyes of the young. Old models were breaking down with no evident replacements, so the psychology of the country was confused and searching. Not surprisingly, the period was marked by the mushrooming of numerous mystical cults, all of which were later swallowed up or eliminated by the Nazi party.

Is the current rise of cults here in North America merely a warning of a broader underlying malaise afflicting the current North American personality? If North America suffers further social disintegration, could she too become ripe for some form of charismatic political movement?

Many people would like to believe that cults are an aberration, a marginal phenomenon whose weirdness makes us feel more comfortable and secure in our own "normality". They take satisfaction in their certainty that "nothing like that could ever happen to me".

But perhaps there is more to be learned from the Boonville experience—extreme and alien as it may seem—than about Moonies or cults. Perhaps cults give us the signs to look for, not just in the outside world, but in ourselves.

And if that is the case, perhaps Boonville might be better seen not only as a place in California, but as a state of mind—a state of mind in which one loses confidence in oneself to such a terrifying extent that one agrees to turn over responsibility for all decisions to an external authority. A process in which, in exchange for solace and certainty, one gives up one's humanness and critical judgement to a person, religion or way of life that offers a simple and easy solution to the complications of life.

This is the conclusion that the authors of the book *Snapping* arrived at after their intensive study of "personality transformation" in cults. They found that people "snap" not only in cults, but in everyday life too, by submitting to grueling work routines, political ideologies, therapies and other systems of rote living that rob them of their personal integrity and humanity.

They concluded that "snapping" is a phenomenon that occurs any time an individual "stops thinking and feeling for himself...and literally loses his mind to some form of external control...as individuality is surrendered to some religion, psychology or recipe for good living that requires no real conscience and no consciousness, no effort or attention on the individual's part.

"Snapping, in all its blind detachment from the world, its disconnection and self-delusion, is a product of a futile attempt on the part of millions of North Americans to escape the responsibilities of being human in this difficult, threatening age."

From this perspective, one can see that there may be many conceivable doors to Boonville: from the religious and from the secular; from the left and from the right of the political spectrum; from broad movements that sweep across a nation to singular, all-consuming love affairs in which one person's identity is swallowed up entirely by the other's.

Anything that one submits to, rather than participates in; acquiesces to rather than challenges, examines, considers and then considers again may have the potential to become a Boonville under the wrong circumstances. As Erich Fromm points out: It is not only *what* one believes in that is important but *how* one believes in it.

Does a person understand who he is and what he is committed to, and adapt and change it according to his own self—or does he simply follow it in good faith wherever it may go? Does he participate in his own life by actively thinking, or does he obey—for if he obeys, it matters little whether he follows Sun Myung Moon, Hitler or the "national interest"—he will be incapable of knowing if his god has failed. And if his god degenerates into irrational and even inhuman behavior, the ever-obedient individual may unknowingly respond with little more humanity or spontaneity than a modern-day cultist.

How can we protect ourselves and our society from this danger? How do we assure that we and our children do not unknowingly slip into similar behavior in the name of some Cause, State or other Messiah?

One way is surely to be aware of the threat, to recognize the frailty of the human, and one's own personality, and be on guard for subtle attempts *by any authorities* to take it over. In Ellul's words, "to show people the extreme effectiveness of the weapon used against them, to rouse them to defend themselves by making them aware of their frailty and their vulnerability."

As my own experience underlines, it is harder to fall into Boonville, if one knows that Boonville exists.

But obviously this is only a stop-gap. The underlying issues go far deeper and strike at the very origin of personality —childhood—and the means we must develop to bring up people to face the responsibilities, and risks, of modern-day freedom. If we cherish our supposed freedom and hope to retain it, how can we encourage our children to be strong enough to use it, brave enough to move about in it without fear? How can we develop people who have enough inner strength so that their values do not begin to crumble as soon as the world around them begins to change?

To equip our children, and ourselves, to meet this challenge is a large, perhaps utopian task. But if we do not soon find a way to begin, perhaps Boonville is not so far away, or half so alien as we may think.

Canadian Appendix

The Unification Church is still in its infancy in Canada, but is growing fast. In 1977, the Church's Canadian wing was almost imperceptible; today it owns more than a million dollars in property and claims over 300 members.

Moonie activities are centred in Quebec and Ontario, particularly Toronto where they have four centres. These include an enormous 42-room house in the Kensington Market area that was acquired for $330,000 in mid-1979. The Church's Ottawa group has bought a large cottage near the University of Ottawa, and the Montreal group recently moved from a run-down inner-city flat to a $110,000 house across the road from the Russian embassy.

The Church also owns Clearstone, a 95-acre estate on Rice Lake near Peterborough that was formerly used by Governor General Vanier. The $270,000 property includes an elegant greystone mansion perched atop a hill, amidst dense forest; the Moonies are constructing a wall around the property. When they purchased Clearstone in 1978, the group said it would be used as a "sheep farm"; instead they are gradually developing it into a Boonville-style training centre.

According to Mike Kropveld, who now operates Cult Information Centre (CIC), an anti-cult research and referral centre, the camp's routine was "pretty slack and ineffective in the first year of operation. But the structure is becoming more and more intense all the time. The seminars still don't rank with Boonville's, but from what we hear, they're definitely getting more sophisticated."

Moon business enterprises in Canada are also growing. The Church operates a posh cosmetic store called Hanida Ginseng Cosmetics in Toronto's Yorkville district. The shop is staffed by glamorous Korean women who sell a variety of potions, lotions and perfumes. Church members also go door-to-door in Toronto and Montreal selling candy, chocolate, peanuts, and dried flowers in glass jars. They often do not identify themselves; if questioned, they say they represent the "Unification Centre".

Moonies also congregate regularly at Toronto's Eaton Centre to recruit members to their Rice Lake camp. The Church's college wing, CARP, recently set up operations on the University of Toronto campus, where they hold weekly Thursday lectures in the Library Science Building.

"The Unification Centre warmly invites you to an evening of discussion and exchange on various subjects relating to social, moral and religious problems today," says a flyer advertising the lectures. Guest speakers are generally officials of the Unification Church.

Another Moon group operating in Canada is the Canadian Unity Freedom Foundation (CUFF), which holds occasional functions in support of federalism. Their PR material makes no mention of the Unification Church. CUFF also turns out a monthly newspaper called *Our Canada*, a small tabloid that takes a strong anti-communist stance.

According to the paper's officials, it has a circulation of some 40,000; however many of these are distributed for free on street corners and at the CBC and U of T. The publisher is identified as simply "Our Canada Publications".

In 1977, a group called the Committee for the International Rally for World Freedom drew a thousand people to a Toronto rally to "mobilize the forces of World Freedom". The event received written endorsements from Premier William Davis, then Toronto mayor David Crombie, and several MP's. Though the rally made no mention of the Unification Church, its officials were all Church members.

Apart from the 300 members living in Canadian centres, several hundred Canadian youngsters are believed to live in U.S. Church centres. Many ex-Moonies say that a sizeable percentage of Moonies throughout the U.S. are Canadian—from cities as diverse as Montreal, Halifax and Vancouver.

As well, Mobile Fund-raising Teams from the U.S. make frequent excursions through Western Canada to sell flowers. During one such trip by Benji, members were told they were "laying the foundation" for a future Boonville-style training camp in the Canadian west.

In the meantime, troops of U.S. Moonies have been seen recruiting members everywhere from Gander, Newfoundland to Vancouver, B.C. California Moonies regularly recruit at Edmonton Airport, offerring to transport potential recruits to a weekend seminar at Boonville, free of charge.

Bibliography

Brown, J.A.C. *Techniques of Persuasion.* Middlesex, England: Pelican. 1963.

Clark, John G. *Manipulation of Madness.* Neue Jugendreligionen. Gotteingen, W. Germany. 1979.

Conway, Flo & Siegelman, Jim. *Snapping.* New York: Delta. 1979.

Crossman, Richard. *The God that Failed.* New York: Bantam. 1952.

Delgado, Richard. *Religious Totalism.* Southern California Law Review. Vol. 51. 1977.

Edwards, Christopher. *Crazy for God.* Englewood Cliffs, N.J.: Prentice-Hall. 1979.

Ellul, Jacques. *Propaganda.* New York: Vintage Books, 1973.

Enroth, Ronald. *Youth, Brainwashing and the Extremist Cults.* Grand Rapids, Michigan: Zondervan. 1977.

Farber, I.E. & Harlow, Harry F. & West, Louis Jolyon. Sociometry. Vol. 20. No. 4. Dec. 1957.

Frank, Jerome D. *Persuasion and Healing.* New York: Schocken books. 1961.

Fraser, Donald. *Investigation of Korean-American Relations.* Report of the Subcommittee on International Organizations. U.S. Government Printing Office. Oct. 31, 1978.

Freed, Josh. *Moonstalkers.* The Montreal Star: Dec. 31, 1977 through Jan. 7, 1978.

Fromm, Erich. *Escape from Freedom.* New York: Avon Books. 1965.

Fromm, Erich. *Psychoanalysis and Religion.* London: Yale University Press. 1950.

Gordon, Suzanne. *Let Them Eat EST.* Mother Jones: Dec. 1978.

Glass, Leonard L. & Kirsch, Michael A. & Parris, Frederick N. *Psychiatric Disturbances associated with Erhard Seminars Training: A Report of Cases; Additional cases and theoretical considerations.* American Journal of Psychiatry: Mar. 77 & Nov. 77.

Hoffer, Eric. *The True Believer.* New York: Harper & Row. 1951.

Hoffer, Eric. *The Ordeal of Change.* New York: Harper & Row. 1963.

Horowitz, Irving. *Science, Sin and Scholarship.* Cambridge, Mass.: MIT Press. 1978.

James, William. *The Varieties of Religious Experience.* Britain: Fontana. 1960.

Koestler, Arthur. *Darkness at Noon.* London: Penguin. 1947.

Kovel, Joel. *Consumer Guide to Therapies.*

Levine, Saul V. *The Role of Psychiatry in the Phenomenon of Cults.* Toronto: 1979.

Fringe Religions: Data and Dilemmas. Toronto. 1979.

Lifton, Robert J. *Thought Reform and the Psychology of Totalism.* New York: W.W. Norton. 1961.

Lofland, John. *Doomsday Cult.* Prentice-Hall. 1976.

Marin, Peter. *Spiritual Obedience.* Harper's magazine. Feb. 1979.

May, Rollo. *Man's Search for Himself.* New York: Delta Books. 1978.

Meerloo, Joost A. *Rape of the Mind.* New York: Grosset & Dunlap. 1961.

Milgram, Stanley. *Obedience to Authority.* New York: Harper & Row. 1974.

Behavioural Study of Obedience, The Journal of Abnormal and Social Psychology. Vol. 67, No. 4, 1963.

Mook, Jane Day. *The Unification Church.* A.D. Magazine: May 1974.

Moon, Sun Myung. *The Divine Principle.* New York: Holy Spirit association for the Unification of World Christianity. 1973.

Master Speaks. Published regularly by the Unification Church. Assembled by Daphne Greene.

Noyes, Dan. *The Thousand Dollar Consciousness.* Mother Jones: April 1979.

Orwell, George. *Nineteen Eighty-four.* Middlesex, England: Penguin. 1954.

Parke, Jo Anne, & Stoner, Carroll. *All God's Children.* Radnor, Pa.: Chilton. 1977.

Patrick, Ted & Dulack, Tom. *Let Our Children Go.* New York: E.P. Dutton. 1976.

Reich, Charles A. *The Greening of America.* New York: Random House. 1970.

Richardson, Herbert W. & Bryant, Darroll W. *A Time for Consideration.* New York and Toronto: Edwin Mellen Press. 1978.

Rogers, Carl. *On Becoming a Person.* Boston: Houghton Mifflin. 1961.

Sargant, William. *Battle for the Mind.* London: Pan Books. 1951. 1959.

The Unquiet Mind. London: Pan Books. 1967.

Shirer, William L. *The Rise and Fall of the Third Reich.* Greenwich, Conn.: Fawcett. 1960.

Shupe, Anson D. & Bromley, David G. *A role theory approach to participation in Religious Movements.* University of Texas at Arlington. 1978.

Sklar, Dusty. *Gods and Beasts: The Nazis and the Occult.* New York: Thomas Y. Crowell. 1977.

Sontag, Frederick. *Sun Myung Moon and the Unification Church.* Nashville, Tenn.: Abingdon. 1977.

Toffler, Alvin. *Future Shock.* New York: Random House. 1970.

Underwood, Barbara & Betty. *Hostage to Heaven.* New York: Clarkson N. Potter. 1979.